MW01180829

Falling in Love 101

Falling in Love 101

A Probe Into Intimacy

The Reverend Edward F. Caldwell

Copyright © 2011 by Edward Caldwell.

Library of Congress Control Number:		2010918851
ISBN:	Hardcover	978-1-4568-3661-0
	Softcover	978-1-4568-3660-3
	Ebook	978-1-4568-3662-7

All rights reserved. No part of this book may be reproduced or transmitted in any form or by any means, electronic or mechanical, including photocopying, recording, or by any information storage and retrieval system, without permission in writing from the copyright owner.

This book was printed in the United States of America.

To order additional copies of this book, contact:
Xlibris Corporation
1-888-795-4274
www.Xlibris.com
Orders@Xlibris.com
90398

Contents

Psalm 78

Part I: *Attendite, popule*

1. Hear my teaching, O my people;*
   incline your ears to the words of my mouth.

2. I will open my mouth in a parable;*
   I will declare the mysteries of ancient times.

3. That which we have heard and know,
   and what our forefathers have told us,*
   we will not hide from their children.

4. We will recount to generations to come
   the praiseworthy deeds and the power of the Lord,*
   and the wonderful works he has done.

5. He gave his decrees to Jacob
   and established a law for Israel,*
   which he commanded them to teach their children;

6. That the generations to come might know,
   and the children yet unborn;*
   that they in their turn might tell it to their children;

7. So that they might put their trust in God,*
   and not forget the deeds of God,
   but keep his commandments;

Author's Preface

I got about halfway through writing the following pages when I started to ask myself, "Why do I write such stuff?" What prompted me originally, I think, was taken from the first seven verses of Psalm 78, which for me, at this point in my eighty-fourth year, touches upon "the legacy" I will be leaving for my four children and four grandchildren—when I am gone! That is the sense I get out of these many words of this Psalm. In addition, when I take into account how my own ancestors—two grandfathers, an uncle, and a great-uncle—wrote about the story of their lives, I began to realize how important and helpful a record of this might be. I suspect some people might not have much interest in knowing what their forbearers wrote about, if anything; perhaps because they put down what they thought their offspring should read. In my case, this is not so. As my ancestors' chronology unravels, there are often little "asides" that tell me they were far from being "stuffed shirts." Hints of their disgruntlement can be detected. I peer *through* the veil that history has closed down upon their "personas (e)." Nevertheless, why would I want to stake out such a vaunted subject as "Falling in Love" that would necessitate something of my own experience of "romantic moments" being disclosed? A slippery slope! For many of you, this becomes a threadbare, silly subject for a clergy person to get himself entangled! All I can say is that any perspective I have culled over the decades might well be worth attention. You will detect elements of autobiography larded into the most solemn asseverations. Actually, what has kept me on focus is that I am writing for two specific people—or is it four? My grandchildren-two are already pretty well grown up, Brody and Cailin—and I am trying to keep in mind as I trudge along Joshua and Emily, currently nine and six. However, it is when they enter the year 2020 that I want them to know something about me-that probably would not be available to them from any other source. Would I dare to think that my ruminations here might emerge as helpful, as I try to imagine what in that year it will be like for them to "take a bow" on the stage of life as late-blooming teenagers! It is them as they will then be that I struggle to address in this memoir. It is more than an exercise in phenomenology—a soliloquy—but a conjectured dialogue, as each of us waits with breathless wonder what the other is thinking! I have just finished reading a terrific book. It is Alan Alda's *Things I Overheard While Talking to Myself.* Let me rephrase this for my own use—for anyone other than members of my own family: "Things Overheard While an Old Grandfather Talks to His Grandchildren." Perhaps herein lay the seeds for a new genre of literature. Therefore, still having a ways to go with "Falling in Love," I move along, hoping that I can finish what I started, but still not really knowing where I will end up.

The Reverend Edward F. Caldwell
October 2010

Romantic Love

Many years ago, a rabbi of the Jewish faith asked me a question: "What is the experience you have of the reality of this Doctrine of Incarnation, which posits the Divine Son Jesus you profess to believe in?" I replied something to the effect that I enjoyed my life in a large cultured historic church downtown, strong on the sacraments and preaching—which gave me a sufficient "encounter" with the person of Christ. My inquirer considered this a religious answer and persisted that if I maintained this "incarnationalism," it should reverberate throughout all the avenues, impressions, expressions of my whole life. This then becomes for me a "prospectus" for my future, and I then sought to "live through" the implications of John 1:14: "And the Word became flesh, and lived among us; and we have seen his glory, the glory as of a father's son full of grace and truth." This proved to be quite a challenge. It meant that I had to dig a little deeper into "little theophanies," where I sensed a convergence of human and divine life. I guessed that one could interpret "incarnation" into physical and psychological dimensions—such as "embodiment," a "presence within," and "a closeness that is intimate."

At that time, what was most probably compelling of interest to me, as a young man in his twenties, was my own experience of "romantic love"! The energy of my sexual urges was filtered through the usual fantasies and anxieties of the unmarried. There were "courtly" as well as earthly components of my imagined, as well as actual trysts, assignations, escapades. (Really now, my purported "love affairs" were so few, I think I remember every single one). Time slipped by with its usual "inevitable," to turn my own involvement in romantic love into a happy marriage and the raising of a wonderful family.

The experience of being a family man encompassed the special relationship Dorothy and I had between ourselves, as husband and wife.

3

Its significance for me continued to unfold weekly over the years until her death ten years ago. Surely, "falling in love" as well as just "being in love" ricochets and weaves itself in refreshing ways whatever other agendas might claim our attention. The only way I felt I might write about this, and make some sense of it because it is laden with so many overtones, was to give it the identity as a "memoir." Many decades now, I have felt baffled and challenged in staking out a theology of some kind through the lens of "romantic love." I have come to realize that two other authors, who likewise have pursued this theme and have written about it most adequately, have immensely helped me. The first is Mary MacDermott Shideler who wrote *The Theology of Romantic Love: A Study in the Writings of Charles Williams.*[1] The second book is *The Novels of Charles Williams* by Howard T. Thomas, especially in his introduction.[2] Contained in the mystery of the doctrine of the incarnation are two principles at least-prototypes-doctrines. The first is that of "co-inherence" and the second is that of "substitution." We probably could add the idea of "exchange." The Divine Word is made "flesh" as we just read. The Divine Word co-inheres in God the Father, as well as in God the Son (Christ), as well as in God the Holy Spirit, which patterns the basis of our belief as Christians. He, Christ, injects his manhood into sacred mysteries of both the incarnation and atonement. The principle of the passion is that he gave his life "for," "on behalf of" the sins of humankind. St. Paul in Galatians 2:19-20 declares, "I have been crucified with Christ, and it is no longer I who live, but it is Christ lives in me. And the life I now live in the flesh I live by faith in the Son of God, who loved me and gave himself for me."

We are constantly being drawn out to comprehend what this means for each of us in the very rough and tumble of our daily lives. In addition, we are called to do so in terms of the Summary of the Law (Matt. 22:34-40) wherein we are enjoined to love God "with all your heart, with all your soul, and with all your mind" and "to love your neighbor as yourself."

It is important to follow the development of the doctrine of the incarnation concerning Christ. This specifies the intention of God to enter into his creation, thus affirming the goodness and value of the created order. It begins with the commonplace actuality of a man-Jesus, who has a double derivation-one directly from God, and one from the created world. The first underlies the fact of decision by God (as Pure Spirit) "to unite himself with matter"—which is done in a mode which involves his creatures to experience joy and ecstasy? The second derivation is at least through his mother. (Williams's understanding of "co-inherence" raises some interesting questions.) He says, "At the beginning of life in the natural order is an act of substitution and co-inherence. A man can have no child unless his seed is received and carried by a woman; a woman can have no child unless she receives and carries the seed of a man—literally, bearing the burden. It is not only a mutual act; it is a mutual act of substitution by the father. The child itself for nine months literally co-inheres in its mother: there is no human creature that has not sprung from such a period of such interior growth." (See also Wisdom of Solomon 7:1-7.) At least here, through the mother, there can be included "projected" into Jesus the whole evolutionary legacy of humankind, the data of intergenerational activity, as well as the cultural and social matrix into which he was born, and thus receives life into himself as within a time frame. One might add, "like the rest of us."

As we follow the progression of Williams's thought, we see how he sets forth a principle, which is one of the most important "building blocks" of life—which is that we are what we are, who we are, because of others. This came to his attention, as it would, during World War I and II—realizing that the peace at home was made possible by the military sacrifices of young men and women. Williams coupled the idea of "exchange" with two other ideas—"substitution" and "co-inherence." Up and down the scale of life, he found that there is no such thing as life that does not owe itself to the life and labor of someone else. To quote Thomas T. Howard, "from the self-giving of a man and woman to each other; to where I find courtesies such as a door open if I have a package; and law obliging me to wait at this red light while you go; and commerce in which I buy what your labor has supplied; right on through nature with its grains of wheat planted and harvested and animals slaughtered for my food; to the highest mystery of all in which a life was laid down so that we might all have eternal life."[3]

Whatever the process of redemption, salvation, would have issued from a general theological perspective, Christians cannot sidestep or evade the inclusiveness of the doctrine of the incarnation. For again, what it declares is that God "objectifies" himself in the person of Jesus Christ—in his life, death, and new life—not in a book, not in a "nobody," but a three-dimensional human body partaking in the full range of its psychophysical powers. He was an embodied knower, with the world as "the crucible"—touching him, connecting to him, with himself sharing in the messy mutuality of its own commonality. The incarnation—as the basic premise for points of identity-underscores the dignity and potential goodness of the human body. The incarnation provides, perhaps most importantly, a sense of justice between man and God. "Man is the measure of all things," as Protagoras proclaimed in the fifth century BC. Justice always needs proportion, the right advantage to "weigh the balances." The slippery slopes of polarity await those whose faith stance fixes itself too far on either the divine side or human side of the spectrum. You cannot have proportion, symmetry, without a common term—and that common term comes to prevail in the "co-inherence" of the divine nature and the human nature in the "Son of God." In addition, to introduce the next section of this paper, the incarnation opens the way for men and women to know love by means of their bodies, by means of their own bodies, and not primarily by means of their own bodies, but by each other's. Even the natural enjoyment of sex depends upon enjoying the other rather than only oneself . . .

Falling in Love

If we are in a reflective mood, we probably admit that "falling in love" seems to confront us regularly, inexorably, sometimes to our dismay, but also often to our delight. Mary McDermott Shideler describes the kaleidoscopic character of love. "Sociologists, psychologists, and biologists probe its symptoms; poets and versifiers expatiate upon its manifestations; cartoonists and preachers regard it as open territory. The event is described as ridiculous, sublime, a transitory episode appropriate only for adolescents, a form of temporary insanity, the sole justification for living at any age, normative, normal, abnormal, pathological, and good clean healthy fun."[4]

Shideler raises the question, in the context of reference to Williams's chapter on "The Image of Beatrice" (Dante): Concerning the matter of "falling in love," can the subject be treated seriously? Is it true? Does it have an ontological threshold, with common symptoms? What are some of the moral ambiguities that we must confront—in even talking about it, putting our quest in print? How might it be possible to reaffirm the love ethic of the Christian faith, when so many Christian approaches from the past have proscribed the body and eroticized the soul? I will attempt to answer these questions as we proceed. We do not have to be solemn about it at every turn of the page! In his chapter on "Eros" in "The Four Loves," C. S. Lewis says, "We must not be totally serious about Venus. Indeed we can't be totally serious without doing violence to our humanity."[5] The quality I might wish to convey in this pursuit is that of respect for the specifics we must engage in! It will take no little effort in just defining the terms used. I hope that I do not convey the idea that I am engaging in a subject matter too vast and beyond the limits of a treatise. One could access the resources of ancient Greek mythology, philosophy, biblical history and teachings, patristic diatribes, renaissance poets and troubadours, writers of plays for the last four hundred years. How is one to appraise the "romantic moment"? Might it be that some things have at least the truth of seeming? "Might these experiences be treated as temporary aspects of the mind, or are they accurate perceptions of the nature of the world and humankind?" One can note their birth, their duration, and their disappearance.

There are case studies to illustrate romantic love in both fact and fiction. One hardly knows where to draw the line. One thinks of rather real people-creative people—as well as stellar couples. Great passions weld them together in wonderful ways, often giving rise to turbulent destinies, but not always. One thinks of Jacob and Rachel; David and Bathsheba; Hosea and Gomer; Tobias and Sarah; Cleopatra and Antony; Elizabeth, Princess of Hungary, and Louis IV, Landgrave of Thuringia (thirteenth century); and Abelard and Heloise (twelfth century). We also think of illustrious spiritual partners such as John and Anne Donne (seventeenth century); Catherine and William Blake (nineteenth century); James and Dolley Madison (nineteenth century); Robert and Elizabeth Barrett Browning (nineteenth century); Edward VIII and the Duchess of Windsor, Wallis Warfield Simpson (twentieth century); as well as C. S. Lewis and Joy Davidman.

If we wonder about causality, as something rooted in the psychophysical nature of human beings, there is a new book entitled *The Secret* by Rhonda Byrne,[6] which has the inviting idea that the secret of life is found in the law of attraction between people. Thoughts are "magnetic" in having a frequency. Each one of us is like a human transmission tower. The feeling of love is the highest frequency you can emit. To know what you are thinking, you should ask yourself how you are feeling! Energy flows to where the attention is focused. To make a relationship work, you zero on what you appreciate about the other person. It takes skill to be able to shift from thoughts that are negative, complaining, and hateful, to the sweeping inclusiveness of praise and blessing for everything in the world. Nevertheless, such shifting can rearrange your connection with the universe and break the links that bind you to your past—as well as bring healing to your body! The law of attraction utilizes the free play of images.

One of the best statements I recall reading about the importance of "images" and the functional aspect of imagination that serves our humble need is from Monica Furlong. In her book *Traveling In*, she says, "I cannot see how, if we did not fantasize about the future, we could consider our own potential. Nor, if we did not rehearse the past, how would we know our own identity. Similarly, we have to play in our minds at love, at sex, at motherhood, or fatherhood as careers or talents or achievements before we can know our own myth, and proceed to live it . . . If we try to abolish fantasy or diversion, we find that this does not abolish them, but simply allows them to build up against our door."[7]

Therefore, what might I say about the contemplation of "falling in love" from its incipient stages? What is the common ground from which it springs forth? I suspect that a kind of youthful innocence and blissful euphoria helps to set the stage! Wordsworth could say of himself: "There was a time when meadow, grove, and stream, the earth and every common sight, to me did seem Appareled in celestial light."[8] Something "the other person" does or says, or in whose life's context occurs to have happened-arrests your attention. You linger over the moment more than normally. (I would not, in today's world, limit my definition of "the other person" to either gender or generation, but simply share my own deeply grounded heterosexuality!) I agree with the author of Proverbs 30:19 that to embark upon this kind of exercise is one of the three things "too wonderful for me." Yes, we can shed some light upon "the way of a man with a girl." You begin to look forward to further contacts with this person. You find that she keeps breaking into your consciousness when your mind is on other things. There is a groundswell of her "presence" that takes over when she is near enough for you to "take her in" in her entirety as a person. One is given the thrill of the voyeur, if she allows the centers of her own perceptions to be made known—in reciprocity to your own! Gradually, a "projection" on your part takes place in your mind's eye—and you find that you are not too far from flinging yourself at her feet. She becomes "idealized" and "idolized." You find yourself in dialogue ready to follow her in every anecdote—to sustain her faultless impression upon you! Ripeness comes when you find life intolerable without her investment in you—however partial it may be. Sexuality and spirituality show signs of being intertwined. She feeds your eyes; you really "behold" her! Her eyes and mouth,—the nape in her neck, the turn of her torso, each detail of her body, are woven into an organic unity, intrinsic in its totality, and shines through her bodily visibility. One seeks for clues to be on the same frequency of feelings. To the "smitten," this can be seen as simply tapping "the tip of the iceberg." One does not want to forget the impact of shyness on speech, or the hope that one is able to put modestly courteous gestures into a lexical frame. Where flights of mutuality increase, there comes moments of profound "being in love," which is an intense, thrilling, personal experience. It comes as something suddenly, shatteringly discovered. The lover finds it difficult to slow down or speed up what is happening to him. This is why the terminology "falling in love" is so apt. One literally feels as if the ground under his feet is giving way. He is not balanced, finds himself "floating" on air—dizzily hurled into new continents of experience. One can well imagine that the poet John Donne was not talking just from what he imagined, but what he found actually so, when he said; "License my roving hands, and let them go, before, behind, between, above, below. O my America! My new-found-land, My kingdom, safeliest when with one man man'd, My Myne of precious stones, My Emperie . . . Full nakedness! All joys are due to thee, As souls unbodied, bodies unclothed must be, To taste whole joys."[9]

In addition, as Donne says in his poem, "The Extasie": "Love's mysteries in souls do grow, but yet the body is his book." To believe in the incarnation opens up the way to "know" what love is, by the vehicle of our own bodies, and not just by the means of our own bodies, but also by each other's bodies. The human body is germane to the imagining capabilities we have in our minds, and contains the prevalence of magnetic attraction, rooted in the index of our genitals and breasts. As one matures, beyond adolescence, and often much further into adulthood, one learns to monitor the feelings associated with the pull and tug of sexual appeal. To bypass the body is to shortchange a person becoming an embodied knower. The human body is a patterned universe, a living epigram of virtue in its diverse and complex operations and self-contained systems, and bears "sweet resonance to the spheres of deep heaven" in the inmost being of its compacted power. Self-consciousness must have a bodily place, which it inhabits. It is important that we do justice to the prospect that the most valued force of human nature is the ability to express human affection. It is important to explore the avenues as to how this is to be played out in actual relationships with other people.

A Remote Ideal or
a Flash of Tangible Reality

It is probably here that we look with some detail at the figure of Beatrice, the beloved of Dante Alighieri (1265-1321) as interpreted by Charles Williams in a chapter of the latter's *He Came Down from Heaven*. Here is the account of the Italian poet's own love for her—"La Vita Nuova," and "Il Convivio"—the source of inspiration for most of his literary work. It is Beatrice who accompanies and guides Dante through their journey of "The Paradiso" part of "The Divine Comedy." His contacts with Beatrice Portinari were brief, infrequent when she was young, and she did marry someone else, as he himself did—to Gemma Donati, by whom he had children. As our focus is upon the romantic aspect of love, it is the poets across the centuries who give us the best material, even though what they wrote contains elements of superstition, folklore, and religious data. Much of this is seen as "cold-shouldered by ecclesiastical authorities" and becomes "a stumbling block to puritans." The inflated imagery artists' share can lure one into putting into practice the very operational actions described. To tread such ground could endanger one's soul, but the invitation of great promise still remains. The center or culminating point is usually noted by those very moments in time when romantic sexual intercourse takes place. There is a "process" one goes through when "falling in love." Its beginning can not only be traced in the obscure "long before," but also in the "all of a sudden, right now." The context of conditions and considerations are not always appropriate for the "end point" to take place. That did not occur in this instance in the case of Dante and Beatrice. There is a wholesome "blossoming" that unfolds in each couple that moves beyond simply "animal appetite." One is to take time in "approaches to loveliness." One is overwhelmed by the *stages* of adoration as sensitivities are triggered by sensations emerging throughout the body. With Dante, we are given his own reflections, documented, authenticated, as to "what happens" when you "fall in love." He provides us with a kind of "grid" to be aware of—to note actual occurrences, which resonate as distinct products of experience—which can be described in detail. I wish to use the same enumeration, as does Charles Williams: When the full sweep of the figure of Beatrice falls into view, (1) "there arises a sense of the intense significance, a sense that an explanation of the universe is being offered, only partially understood, however"; (2) "she is the pattern of human excellence (with reference to its divine source), the center and norm of humanity, with others existing so long as they resemble her"; (3) "divine light radiates, emanates, through her, in revelatory acts, which may be called her behavior, carriage; she disseminates glory, that 'true light that enlightens everyone coming into the world'" (John 1:9); (4) "this lady is a thing *visibly miraculous*—appearing with this quality as of something (someone) unaffected by time—indeed she is eternal, the substance of spirit"; (5) the question now arises as to *how* she is to be praised in terms of her body as well as her spirit (soul). "With much pleasure does her beauty feed the eyes of those who behold her . . . ?" Not only forehead and hand are radiant. The beauty of her soul is transparent now in her eyes—limpid, soft; in her mouth, her lips-smiling, laughing, yet conveying a pervasive modesty, humility, innocence! After gazing freely for so long, the observer becomes intoxicated—so dazzling the glory. This can lead the beholder astray. One is to stake out and lay hold of the pattern, the symmetry of the vision, that he not lose touch with any of its parts. (Probably most important of all) "Her beauty has power to renovate nature in those who behold her (when what is conveyed really registers upon the beholder). The ultimate effect can bring about a quickening of one's latent energies, and even reformation, conversion, transfiguration. This includes pardon to restore innocence, and even physical healing. A new vision is given, even though momentarily, as to what their lives would be like—together!" The chief grace she bestows is humility; there is a veritable "self-forgetfulness, which makes room for adoration." That is to say, there is no evidence of struggling, striving, to attain some level of awareness, to enable her to be so generous of spirit. Rather, it is the texture of the union of flesh and spirit in her that makes her accessible to those intimacies. This is what makes her so inviting. She is still an "ordinary girl," but it is her gift of *tangible love*, whether or not it is fully expressed, that makes her so extraordinary.

Williams declares, [10] "Hell has three principle attacks on the Way of Romantic love." The dangerous assumptions are: (1) the assumption that it will naturally be everlasting—that is to say however that though, of course, it cannot be everlastingly 'visible,' its authority can still remain intact. There is a pledged fidelity needed to sustain the life it seeks to give; (2) the assumption that it is personal. It is a mistake to consider the revelation and the glory as one's own personal property. Possessiveness is as the sin of coveting, and gives rise to other sins such as jealousy, envy, and idolatry. A state of sanctity has yet to be achieved. The 'graciousness' of God is the chief sign of both giver and receiver—who have come through and weathered all the trammels of Romantic Love. (3) There is the assumption (false) that such an experience just above described is sufficient. But no! Social duties are to be recognized—even though St. Paul tells us: 'If I give away all my possessions . . . but do not have love, I gain nothing' (1 Cor. 13:3). 'To be in love must be followed by the will to love' (John 1:9). The light that lightens everyone coming into the world is to be seen without as well as within.

The Anatomy of "Falling in Love" — Further Morphology

When one is moving along the path of actually being in love, he finds in himself a not-so-gentle impetus that draws him forward to form, mold, jell something with his hands. The body of the damsel, who is the object of his affections, becomes the instigator of this desire. Her very being is transformed into an icon. Each detail about her is distinctly perceived. Yet the two realities about her in terms of "figure" and "ground" interpenetrate one another. What is numinous, mysterious, partakes of what is sharp, vivid, specific. Yes, it is this girl, having these "curves," this aura about her head and hair, this astonishing geometric swivel to her hips, etcetera, that makes him speechless. The poet Robert Herrick (seventeenth century) describes the cadences of her clothes as well as her body, when she is in motion, even posturing—"a sweet disorder in the dress / Kindles in clothes a wantonness."[11] Nevertheless, we might also include the way she asks the waiter for a pat of butter—"a foot stepping from the train is the rock of all existence." As Williams speaks of Beatrice, the sight of the beloved arouses in Dante, a sense of utter, overpowering significance—"an explanation of the whole universe is being offered, and indeed, understood."[12] She appears to him, not only as good, but also as the visible norm of goodness.[13] Others may know her as a commonplace girl, perhaps a bit lazy, stupid, petulant, but not lover-boy. It is not so much that the vision of perfection overrules imperfection, as much as it simply relegates it to oblivion. Others may not understand a relationship so unique. It is a first-time experience.

Many of us at this point are becoming aware that we are entering into the mode, genre, of images that are part of a book in the Hebrew Scriptures, in a section of its Wisdom Literature—"The Song of Songs." There are repeated descriptions of the woman, the country girl (shepherdess)—4:1-7;

6:4-9; 7:1-6—in which parts of the body are singled out; each part of the body is compared to a different object with which it shares one trait. For moderns, some of this can sound corny, whimsical! "The Song of Songs" is indeed "the best of the best," the most superlative song that could be ever sung! Yet for all its brevity, when we read it, it leaves us puzzled, frustrated. Some of this has to do with its internal structure. It is best seen as a series of poems strung together; its verses are all composed of direct, personal address, a series of dialogues, which gather momentum, with no little repetition. The other factor affecting its actual helpfulness has to do with the complex thought patterns we bring to it and hence impose upon it. Across the centuries, it has been taken hostage by allegorists. When it comes to sex, we have an overlay of assumptions, presumptions, which are hard to disentangle. For me, it is important to stake out at the start, from *The New Interpreter's Bible Study*,[14] the claim: "Today, biblical scholarship of whatever stripe generally recognizes a literal sense that celebrates a wholesome sexual relationship between man and woman. The text poetically expresses the spiritual values of fidelity, mutuality, and fervor of human love in agreement with the goodness of God's creation. (Gen. 1-especially verse 31—"God saw everything that he had made, and indeed, it was very good.)"

Marcia Falk, in the preface to her translation of "The Song . . ."[15] highlights the character of its contents, which make it pertinent to the experience of "falling in love." She says, "females speak over half the lines . . . they speak out of their own experiences . . . that do not seem filtered through the lens of patriarchal consciousness . . . women and men alike share a range of emotionally expressive action and language; women initiate lovemaking at least as often as men; both female and male voices are at times urgent and assertive . . . vulnerable and tender. Even the metaphors to describe the lovers' bodies shatter stereotypes; both speakers remark upon their beloved dovelike eyes . . . in the text a man is described as having cheeks like spices, lips like lilies. In the Song no domination exists between the human beings and the rest of nature . . . Depictions of nature—as metaphor, context, and motif—abound, and nature appears in the richness of its myriad manifestations. The Song is all the more remarkable for its emotional complexity and depth . . . conflicting emotions interlace in the poems; anxiety, loss, frustrations, and even hostility are interwoven with erotic and sensual joys."

In my attempt to give "content" to the experience of "falling in love," there comes the time when we must consider the "time frame" about what we are talking. There is not much evidence in "The Song" that is helpful—all that transpires here could do so in several weeks. Romantic love in its devotees, at least initially, seeks to embrace the various rhythms of life, its peaks and valleys—always as something new to share with one another. Moments of quiet affection, gentle serenity, are seen to have as much value as times of dashing about, exciting escapades, high adventure, anything to ensure the authentic making of one available to the other. Through untrammeled runs of self-disclosure, the lover yearns to narrow "the distance" between himself and his beloved. He forges through into the "unknown" to discover all that he can possibly learn about her, not just to satisfy his own curiosity, but to awaken the complete person in her. When reciprocated (by her), the confluences of these energies emerge, ecstasy erupts, and we behold the transcendence that ripples out into the world, the echo of which we hear in "love songs" from time immemorial: "Earth's crammed with heaven and every common bush afire with God." However, in all this, is it possible to say there is a certain sequence of development normally associated with the unfolding of lovemaking—"arresting notice," infatuations, and enchantment—and then, either commitment or severance?

"The Song of Songs" as I have indicated, is not easy to understand, though an abundance of ordinary words appears in every line. Most often, we come to read it, in order to figure out where and how they are "having" sex! There are shifts in speakers, oscillations in mood. Soliloquy alternates with colloquy. Various feeling tones emerge in adjuration, rhapsody, and simple meditation, which can include grief. That this scripture deserves our unhurried scrutiny becomes evident, as we piece together the few pieces of autobiography that surface—in the principal people involved. There is more disclosure concerning the girl than the boy, and probably much to suggest ad hoc impressions. There is their awareness of the social situation, the context, in which their love affair plays itself out. The girl shares the fact of her lover with her maidens. Her own self-appraisal that she is "black and beautiful" can reflect a condition that her brothers have imposed on her—putting her to work in the vineyard. It is a statement of accountability! We are left wondering whether this is an asset or liability in the eyes of her companions: "Will you disrobe me with your stares?" suggests she is not entirely happy with their scrutiny. The officious brothers reappear at the end in chapter 8 verses 8-10—their role in overseeing their sister's activities—is met by her affirming her own maturity, and the peace she has been given by her lover, and that she alone now can dispose of her own vineyard—that is her body! Others do have an influence in her life (mostly for good). She realizes the consequences of her actions, all the while feeling free to be transparent about her most moving affections, but also able to qualify them, and even have reservations about where her thoughts may lead her.

Daphne Merkin, author[16], editor, is critical of "The Song." She admits its obvious suggestiveness, that it is "lyrical, yes, intimate and charming, but not particularly sexy." She attributes this to "the rusticity of the amorous imagery" and that "the moorings of identity are too tentative, too amorphous." In addition, that it is "a zookeeper's vision of loveliness."

Phyllis Trible, author and professor, in her book *God and Rhetoric of Sexuality*[17] approaches "The Song . . ." from the angle of what happened in Genesis 2 and 3 (The Garden of Eden, The First Sin and Its Punishment). She uses these stories as her hermeneutical key to unlock the symbolism in this garden, from which man and woman were sent forth and excluded, and uses them as clues for entering this second Garden of Eden, "The Song of Songs." She notes, as have our previous authors, the series of metaphors, "in which many meanings intertwine," and in which "love itself blends sight, sound, sense, and non-sense." As we may have noticed, God does not speak here, nor is deity even mentioned. The prime motifs—of the search, the watchmen, and the mother's house—surface in cyclical combinations. Here are distinct "movements" in this Symphony of Eros—with parallelism in structure and content. The maiden speaks much about her lover while on her search and then directly when they are coming together, as in 3:1-3 and 8:1-3, 6, 7, 14. Her first words invite us to enter this circle of intimacy, but her last tell us to go! Just as male and female become "one flesh" in the Garden of Eden (Gen. 2:24), so now the lovers themselves praise the joys of intercourse. "My garden" and "his garden" blend in mutual habitation and harmony, and in a saturation of the senses. Embrace confirms the delights of "touching." Here the births of lovers are linked to mothers. Eros is inclusive, for the love between the two welcomes the companionship of many. There is no assertion of one over the other. Love is so powerful that no even the primeval waters of chaos can destroy Eros (Gen. 1:1, 2). Neither escaping from nor exploiting sex, they celebrate "one flesh." Never is the woman called wife, never is she requested to bear children. On issues of marriage and procreation, "The Song . . ." says naught. Love for the sake of love is its message!

After spending so much time with women authors, let us hear from a man—his assessment of "The Song . . ." In Michael R. Cosby's *Sex in the Bible,*[18] he includes a chapter on this twenty-second book in the Bible—with an addition to the title, "A Celebration of the Sensuous." As I was reading what he wrote, he gives me the feel of a male's point of view! He wonders about the frankness—that here indeed we encounter "a sea of emotional expression," "open eroticism." As with others, he notes the sudden, abrupt, changes of settings, characters, speakers. Then, not taken aback by the "amorphous," he asks incisively as to how we moderns would look at the situation if we were participants in the same setting! His concern is with the actual use of language, the use of image, to describe what is seen, heard, touched, fondled—in lovemaking ("pillow talk!"). As a part of this, he identifies those times when the young man not only affirms his intention to make love to his beloved, looking forward to a new experience, but also the specific times in the narration. So there is not only a "first time" (4:9-5:2), but also "through the night" (2:17; 7:8, 9, 12, 13)—this time having now an intimate knowledge of her body.

Praising beauty turns into simple "flattery as foreplay." However, in the various special alignments of "where they are with one another," Cosby, for me, suggests the possibility of an emerging predatory nature prevalent in both of them. Cosby seems to be more perceptive as to "when" sexual intercourse takes place. I tend to agree with him, as we gather in chapter 7, with the young man getting pretty excited when "he observes her nicely curved thighs (as) like the beautiful work of a master artist . . . like a well-proportioned statue"—"Your navel is a rounded bowl that never lacks mixed wine. Your belly is a heap of wheat, encircled with lilies." So it is that the man comments on "the intoxicating things which her navel (vulva) holds for him, for it is the hollow shape of a drinking glass."

In a sense, it could be said that all the allusions, images recorded here have their source, not in immediate verbal response, but in reminiscence, reflection, and are second-hand. We become aware of the transition from "a garden locked, a fountain sealed" (4:12) to "a garden fountain, a well of living water . . . flowing streams" of (4:15) as implying the presence of continuity in all the delicacies imaginable, as extended in time—of every possible pleasure. Does the verbalization of all this become necessary? Perhaps so. Feelings are aroused in every other part of the body to such intensity—that to speak with the tongue—other than a "shout" of exclamation would be simply a distraction. Communication takes place on completely other wavelengths!

Three times in 3:1-4, she imagines herself seeking "him whom my soul loves" for a tryst, and qualifies this in 2:7, "do not stir up or awaken love until it is ready!" also in 3:5, "do not stir up or awaken love until it is ready!" and again in 8:4, "do not stir up or awaken love until it is ready." The moment is more than a "knee-jerk" reaction. Love is to be allowed to ripen to its full bloom—for its fullest expression. The image of the "dove" in their reference to each other's eyes (probably) (1:15 and 5:2) symbolizes purity, gentleness, fidelity. In extolling the beauty of she whom the young man loves, he speaks of her sexuality as "a garden locked is my sister, my bride, a garden locked, a fountain sealed (4:12)." The emphasis here is upon both her modesty, exclusiveness, and points to his desire to enter. It highlights Proverbs 5:15-18: "Drink water from your own cistern, flowing water from your own well. Should your springs be scattered abroad, streams of water in the street? Let them be for yourself alone, and not for sharing with strangers. Let your fountain be blessed, and rejoice in the wife of your youth." The theme of modesty is present in the fact that the lovers are always seeking some place—a clandestine setting—where they can have their own privacy, and not be so public in their affections. (5:6-8; 6:1; 8:1, 1) The poems here flagrantly celebrate physical love, and yet it is apparent that how and where that love is exercised are neither coarse, vulgar, lewd.

"The Song" does not disclose questions we might naturally wonder about the couple. As the intensity of their love for one another is set forth, we do not know what actually has brought them together other than their love for one another. There can be gradations in love as we hear from the story of Jacob in Genesis 29, who loved Laban's daughter Rachel more than his daughter Leah. As we know in our own "love life," there can be subsidiary reasons for why we love a certain someone more than someone else! Love is not uncaused, but it can be subject to spontaneity, accompanied by self-deprecatory feelings. As here, in "The Song," the maiden can think of herself as unworthy because she is "swarthy." We know there may be relationships that transcend a sense of merit or worth in the other. Chapter 8 verses 6-7 have one of the clearest expressions, almost by definition, of romantic love, in highlighting its power, its "fierceness." "Set me as a seal upon your heart, as a seal upon your arm; for love is strong as death, passion as fierce as the grave. Its flashes are flashes of fire, a raging flame. Many waters cannot quench love; neither can floods drown it . . ." Elizabeth Barrett Browning in her "Sonnets From the Portuguese" gives us a touch of what it is like to live and value this rare atmosphere:

> If thou must love me, let it be for naught
> Except for love's sake only. Do not say

'I love her for her smile . . . her look . . . her way
Of speaking gently . . . for a trick of thought
That falls in well with mine, and certes brought
A sense of pleasant ease on such a day'-
For these things in themselves, Beloved, may
Be changed, or change for thee,
and love so wrought,
May be unwrought so. Neither love me for
Thine own dear pity's wiping my cheeks dry,
A creature might forget to weep, who bore
Thy comfort long, and lose thy love thereby.
But love me for love's sake, that evermore
Thou may'st love on through love's eternity.[19]

The text from "The Song" surely suggests the possibility of "love sickness," which refers to someone so much in love as to be unable to act in a normal way. Several translations of "The Song" have marginal notes to indicate the assumption that when sexual intercourse is mentioned, it is meant to occur within the parameters of marriage. It is not difficult, given all the allusions in the text, to slip into a wedding-bride and groom context. However, as I read it, the making sure that they are married does not strike me as its primary purpose. It does raise the question as to the circumstances of their consummating their relationship. That question does not seem to arise as requiring a decision to be made. Nevertheless, it can be an important one for a couple who "fall in love."

In order to "thicken the soup," I would like to have recourse to another biblical story—the account of the patriarch Joseph and Potiphar's wife in Genesis 39. But in a moment!

"Falling in love" includes the "riding along on the crest of a wave" in which "lovemaking" emerges as a "symphony of experience infinitely complicated in meaning." An extremely desirable state to be able to maintain, but it is just not in our nature to "show up," manifest, this side of ourselves, in most circumstances throughout a typical day. Erotic passion cannot be sustained, and even when in anticipation, you stake all your bets on "fulfilled desire," one quickly loses interest in the actual event, once it is passed. For most of us, romantic passion does not reach the heights seemingly scaled in "The Song of Songs." It might even be compared with the manna in the wilderness for the Israelites (Ex. 16:20) in references to what is transitory, ephemeral. From the heat of the day, when it passes, it "bred worms and turned foul." In 2 Samuel 13, we are presented with a case of a father who does not punish his daughter's rapist, and a brother who takes vengeance, and thus earns the father's anger—King David and Tamar Absolom's full sister. Amnon manipulates David in sending Tamar, for a meal, feigning illness. Amnon imitates his father David in taking what he wants with impunity. But he has not learned of David's repentance! Having raped her, Amnon wants nothing more to do with her (verse 15), "he was seized with a very great loathing for her." We are aware of how our feelings can vacillate—even back and forth—across a wide spectrum of emotions—from a variety of causes—tiredness, just being out of sorts, carrying some burden or grief, which gnaws at our consciousness. In terms of a psychological paradigm through which we might look at our situation, it is important at times to consider the demonic aspect of some relationships, which can poison, infect some couples in courtship. That does not auger well for their future. The love of one for another can be tainted by a rigid self-defensive system, with constant recourse "to control" that ultimately restricts the freedom of the other to be the agent of his or her own actions. This curtails, diminishes the person so treated to live spontaneously, imaginatively, creatively!

Rollo May, in his book *Love and Will* describes the elements of the "new Puritanism" in our so-called emancipated, liberated world. His words, printed in 1969 still apply! We have three anthropological problems: (1) Influences, which alienate us from our bodies, (2) the ways we separate emotion from our reasoning, cerebral powers, and (3) our use and treatment of our body as a machine. These are basic impediments internal to one's psychological caste that make "falling in love" a problem or at least an issue, where two people in a relationship are concerned. The human body teaches us that our sexuality is not to be separated from other physical expressions of our being—that everything is a part of our unique fleshly signature.[20] Muse upon a phrase from James Joyce's "Ulysses": "Mr. Duffy lived just a short distance away from his body." It is easier than not in our modern world to be "fragmented" by the rift between abstract thought and the "hardened forms" of the material world, with all its multifarious expressions even with the soft internal parts of our own bodies. The revelations of God indeed not only may break into life from heaven (outside of our world), but also include the indwelling of the supernatural, growing up and out of the particular context in which our bodily selves find themselves. Our soul must lay claim to that sense of feel that dwells in all the parts of our bodies. One loves another from the web of mystery in the magnetic field of attraction that holds us together, as subject, object, and as the ground by which we "form a secret partnership with possibility." In Psalm 85, we read, "Truth shall spring up from the earth, and righteousness shall look down from heaven?" Time and again, it can be seen from the broad work of counselors in our society that one can drift into becoming a robotlike individual, aloof, detached, superior, out-of-touch, spaced-out—one whose capacity to really feel has been shredded.

What has become a challenge to me in writing about falling in love is how I could use the Bible as my basic resource to identify those situations in which a couple—man and woman—are thrown together. With those stirrings of love that begin to emerge one way or another, there seems to follow a process to be gone through. The story of the courtship of Isaac and Rebekah is the product of Abraham using his servant to return to the ancestral home "to get a wife for my son, Isaac" (Gen. 24:4). The contact that King Solomon had with the Queen of Sheba (1 Kings 10) indicates more was going on here than just a state visit. She comes "to test him with hard questions. When she came to him, she told him all that was upon her mind; there was nothing hidden from the king that he could not explain to her. When the Queen of Sheba had observed all the Wisdom of Solomon [and all his grandeur], there was no more spirit in her . . . King Solomon gave the Queen of Sheba every desire that she expressed, as well as what he gave her (out of his royal bounty.) Then she returned to her own land, with all her servants" (1 Kings 10:1-14).

From the sexual irregularities of old Judah and his daughter-in-law Tamar in Genesis 38, we pick up again with the story of Joseph in chapter 39. Much has happened to young Joseph thus far. He has already been through the furnace of adversity, hardship, affliction from his own family, especially his brothers. Rescued from the pit, sold as a slave, transported to Egypt, he enters into the employ of Potiphar prince, an office of Pharaoh. Here I would follow the painstaking account in detail—the 1,200-page volume of Thomas Mann's "Joseph and His Brother."[21] As a brilliant youth, Joseph gradually emerges from his lowly state and becomes recognized for his visible handsomeness, his golden bronze shoulders, as well as his good graces and executive ability. What is so intriguing in Mann's account is that he cites *seven* reasons for Joseph not having sexual intercourse with Potiphar's wife when she "cast her eyes on him and said, 'Lie with me'" (verse 7). Resisting her blandishments, he abstains from taking her. We do not know from his point of view whether this was a difficult, unmanageable thing to do—not to respond to her intimate overtures of affection, which were repeated "day after day" (verse 10). Joseph was a virile, whole man—whose own chastity figures mainly in this part of the narrative. The two principal characters here Potiphar, who is impotent (castrated as a child?) honorary husband of Mut-em-enet, who is his chief wife. Here we see how the ground could be laid for her pining for a man, to become enamored of Joseph. Mention is made of the insistence, intensity of this temptation—his continuous refusal of her advances-(verses 8, 9)—he said to his master's wife "Look, with me here . . . my master has put everything that he has in my hand . . . he has kept (nothing) back from me except yourself, because you are his wife. How then could I do this great wickedness, and sin against God?" Then, as we know, she puts him into the position of making it appear that he was trying to seduce her. Potiphar may suspect the truth for he sends Joseph off to rather lenient imprisonment.

From what we know of Joseph at this point, it could be said that though he began life as the "darling" of his father, he does emerge from the bosom of a dysfunctional family. He is able to draw upon the respect of those he is thrown in contact with. He might have every reason to appeal to self-pity—to justify his passions. Though of a compliant spirit (he could be in love with everything) still, he was mindful of his spiritual inheritance, which Mann identifies as his first reason, for "no sex." He was aware of his "bride ship with God"—the covenant of circumcision—by which one is selected, chosen of God. In this selective process, there could be a touch of jealousy by the one choosing! The second reason, as we have already read, is his loyalty to the master, Potiphar. He had been entrusted with all the affairs of the household. Besmirching this trust could affect his position. Thirdly, he would be the "arrow"—not the goal of desire—it could be considered a touch of male vanity, but he was not going to woo a woman who behaved as a man! The fourth reason was clearly a rejection of his slave status—for to "mingle his blood with hers" would simple reinforce what he was in her eyes, but not in his own. The fifth reason had to do with Joseph's own father—Jacob—and the suspicions that had come from him about the people of the land who had "infected themselves with wantonness." In matters of morality and personal discipline, anything and everything was allowed—there was no accountability to a "higher power." The sixth reason came down to the very practicalities by which he lived through the hours of each day. The God of Joseph was a God of "Spirit," not an idol, not something fixed in a dead image of wood or metal—as of those objects of Baal. Finally, the last reason was to be identified as "the fear of laying himself bare." There was that accursed affair with Noah in his tent, when he became drunk and "lay uncovered in his tent" (Gen. 9:21, 22), "and Ham . . . saw the nakedness of his father." Mindful would Joseph be of how Reuben lost his firstborn status in Jacob's last works to his sons: "Unstable as water, you shall no longer excel . . . because you went up onto your father's bed" (Gen. 49:3 and 35:22) "and lay with Bilhah his father's concubine"—a penalty that still could hover over Joseph's head.

This one example of Joseph's relationship with Potiphar's wife impressed me, because (according to Thomas Mann) there could be so many causes to explain Joseph's responses—to something that genuinely entices him—almost. Her love for him was not reciprocated! There is still suggested the fact that he felt he could play the game of venturing into danger and retreating at will. His haughtiness of spirit coupled with a sense of his own self-indulgent mockery of his inviolability was balanced by his desire to lose nothing of himself, and to do no harm to anyone else.

The complexity of his response is so evident here. However, could we add any considerations of our own these many of hundred of year later? Those of us who still live with some of the basic proprieties of courtship always want to make room for a relationship to exercise its togetherness within a period of months and even years. Every relationship between two people, whoever they are, to one another, has a bodily aspect to it. This, as we know, is crucial in mother and child—with the mother as agent, and the child as recipient, and for all the rest of us that we may develop a sound sense of our own bodies.

In terms of adults, we face the multi-faced character that resides in every one of us. Our personas can manifest different ego—identities, varied archetypal images, charlatan shadow-sides—each often elicited by various contexts of circumstances! Every human relationship may turn out to be either negative or positive. There is *a love and a hate in every* relationship—a desire to be affectionate, helpful, and a desire to destroy, cast away. Each of us can reflect upon our own varied expressions of our own psychological states—even across the hours of a single day! It is important to ask ourselves—what is to be our approach to other people—in whatever intimacy we share with them in space? We do have a window of choice in this matter, though sometimes it may be minimal. The importance of having a good disposition is never to be ignored. One is to be as loving as possible and act out of a spirit of good will. The need for this casts into bold relief one's recourse to prayer. For me, the most important prayer in the Book of Common Prayer is the Collect for the Seventh Sunday after the Epiphany, which reads,

O Lord, you have taught us that without love whatever we do is worth nothing: Send your Holy Spirit and pour into our hearts your greatest gift, which is love, the true bond of peace and of all virtue, without which whoever lives is accounted dead before you.[22]

The language of this prayer is lifted from the First Letter of Paul to the Corinthians—chapter 13. What is sharply defined in these references is what constitutes the absence of love in any human situation, and that is death, the utter negation of everything, extinction.

We are to persist in tracking down the secrets of our own identity in life. This takes place not only when we are reflective about our past, our hopes, and ourselves for the future, but also it takes place when we are willing to interact with all kinds of people. There is a real case for saying that everyone with whom we converse face-to-face is, in part, a mirror to ourselves and for ourselves even when there are differences. We are always vulnerable in this context. The effect and affect of changes in "self-image" taking place is subtle and hardly noticeable, but it occurs even during the smallest bits of self-revelation. The impact others have upon us is tremendous.

Here I would make a statement about myself, my own character that central thrust of a constellation of traits, which to my best knowledge constitutes "me"! Here I touch the marrow of my being, unbarred. If we have lived with ourselves a whole number of years, we should, by the time we have gray hairs, have arrived at a point in life when the depth of our feelings are sufficiently integrated with the way we wish to present ourselves to others. Even astrological insights can be helpful here. (I am a Taurus, born May 1, 1926.) I am a warmhearted, benign individual who has not only been blessed with a good disposition, but also have a fascination about other people. I am curious about them, even eager for them to tell me how they live. It takes some blatant offense to get my temper riled up! I know I function best in an atmosphere where there is harmony, peace, and contentment. My desire for friendship with others does not rule out my discernment of their shortcomings, their limitations, their infirmities. These things are not seen by me as grounds to flaunt my superiority over them, but as eliciting from me feelings of pity, sympathy, and the desire to heal and to help. When I awake each morning, my first thought is to deal with the realization of the miracle of my own life. This surely is not a strange thought to any of us. We have but to consider "all the things I have had to go through." The first and foremost prayer I seem in need of saying each day is taken from Psalm 51, verse 11:

> Create in me a clean heart, O God, and renew a right spirit within me." Help me to meet with quiet confidence whatever trials the day holds and strengthen me against temptation.

I've had to learn to be honest about myself over a vast expanse of time. I have been a widower now for ten years; Dorothy and I were together—as a married couple—for forty-nine years. I live with my eldest son. For reasons that become apparent in the reading of this monograph, I do not like to live out my days and the hours of my days very long apart from the presence of women. As if it were ground genetically into my very being, that to simply look at most women, my whole body tingles with excitement. It makes life worth living another day. The author John O'Donohue, who wrote the book, *Beauty the Invisible Embrace*, immensely helps me. He says this, "Eros is a divine force. It infuses all the earth. Yet too often, in our own culture Eros is equated with lust and sexual greed. However, it is a more profound and sacred force than this. Eros is the light of wisdom that awakens and guides the sensuous. The energy illuminates the earth. Without it, the earth would be a bare, cold planet . . . Amidst the vast expanse of fields and seas; the providence of Eros awakens and sustains the longing of the earth. This is the nerve source of all attraction, creativity, and procreation. Eros is the mother of life, the force that has brought us here. It kindles in us the flame of beauty and the desire for the Beautiful as a path towards growth and transformation" (page 152, 3). Adding to this comment, we are to be aware of the presence of Eros in our own lives, as on page 43: "While the Beauty of nature awakens and fills our senses, the Eros of the human mind always desires to make a deeper voyage and explore the forms in which beauty dwells among us."[23] Beauty is something that enables us to live between "the act of awakening and the act of surrender." Glamour is no substitute for Beauty; nor is the rushed heart or arrogant mind. It is not enough to live just in the imperative of the "stand alone," "the digital instant, or the mechanical mind—with its singular focus. Any image with its braided and luminous moments should have the capacity to surprise us. The lives of those we know, need, and love, all dwell behind faces—the more symmetrical the face, the more beautiful it is, and it is just by such we discover the hidden geometry and harmony of the human mind. This becomes ever so clearer to us when presented with a smile, which can completely transform a face.

Those of us, both young and old, who are Christian, and find ourselves living amid quandaries—not a few—because we find ourselves somewhere in that state of having fallen in love, we naturally feel led to turn to the scriptures—specifically, the New Testament! Both the person of Jesus Christ, his teachings and example, as well as the reported experiences of the first disciples and their counsel, we would assume provide helpful guidelines, as we find to be true in other concerns of life. This is actually not quite so! There are negative texts that can make it difficult for a Christian to accept his or her own sexuality openly, without guilt or fear. These can be bedrock declarations that make it difficult to assimilate our own experiences into a holistic Christian vision of life. Judaism is more fruitful in this regard with such affirmations as are found in the Jerusalem Talmud; "Every person will have to give an account for every pleasure in this world which he did not partake of."[24] Christian love, on the other hand, does not well survive transition into the bedroom!

So much depends on how we are to interpret given texts. To approach this sensitive subject (and here I hope I am not going a long way 'round to prove a point), I would like to simply look at 1 Peter 3:3-4. The counsel is addressed to wives. "Do not adorn yourselves outwardly by braiding your hair, and by wearing gold ornaments or fine clothing; rather let your adornment be the inner self with the lasting beauty of a gentle and quiet spirit, which is very precious in God's sight."

The first thing we see here is the issue of vanity, and the second is that the clothing and countenance are meant to communicate the genuine personhood of the woman within. She is obviously not to be slovenly. I think what I am looking for is probably a more modern term than I realize—and that word is "charm." What captures the essence of a woman's beauty is contained in the word "charm." This defines that quality or feature that attracts, delights, enchants, a (male?) spectator—sometimes by magic by the casting of a spell. I would contend that this is a rare attribute to be discerned in the New Testament, so we are not to be unduly judgmental. Some may feel this is a peripheral, modern concern. The specifics of this text in verses 3 and 4, at least in what it points to particular people, whose lives we encounter across the pages of the New Testament, I come up with a category empty of instances. (In the Hebrew Scriptures, the story of Esther, in the book after her name—the regimen she was required to endure to become queen to King Ahasuerus gives a clue as to how she must have appeared in public. However, this is a tale in a pagan world.) The only other instance of charm personified is in the Book of Judith (Apocrypha) in chapter 10, which tells of how Judith, a woman known for her piety and beauty, prepares herself in an attractive manner with all the aids, which wealth and cosmetics could provide, in order to set the stage for the deceit she is about to practice against Holofernes, the general for Nebucachadnezzer. Her ruse is to obtain privacy in his tent and then kill him by beheading him!

Many saints come to mind in the New Testament, and they exhibit stellar qualities—heroic faith, basic goodness, service to others, even holiness of life. We see them from the outset of Jesus's own commissioning of disciples. There are those who have been healed, whose lives were changed by their conversion, whose own ministry was set in motion—such as the Samaritan woman at the well in John 4, Mary Magdalene in Luke 8:1-3 and John 20:1-18. With some, there can be one feature, like hospitality, that stands out—Mary and Martha of Bethany in Luke 10:38-42, John 11, Dorcas in Acts 9:36—her "good works and acts of charity," and Lydia in Acts 16:11-15, "come and stay at my home."

It is not easy to factor in what we can know today of women's role and function in biblical times. It takes thoughtful perception to see their "visibility" in narrative and letters—the specifics of this "visibility" colored by their unique traits and character. Given our own tremendously enriched visual orientation through TV, movies, etc., we must remember that back then "to be seen"—what we would see—would be qualifiedly different. Such things as communal functioning under the commandment—"Thou shalt not make to thyself any graven image"—no "mirroring" though indeed there could be pieces of statuary, mosaics nearby! It is hard for us to visual what women looked like in their daily housekeeping routines. The general attitude toward women in that covenanted society was strongly affected by male dominance—father, husband, and brother. In Jewish society, women's basic identity came from their being property, chattel (Ex. 20:17).

There is a paragraph in the Sermon on the Mount that disturbs me. Jesus is teaching, and it is familiar to most of us: "You have heard that it was said, 'You shall not commit adultery.' But I say to you that everyone who looks at a woman with lust has already committed adultery with her in his heart. If your right eye causes you to sin, tear it out and throw it away; it is better for you to lose one of your members than for your whole body to be thrown into hell. And if your right hand causes you to sin, cut it off and throw it away; for it is better for you to lose one of your members than for your whole body to go to hell" (Matt. 5:27-30).

The first thing that strikes us about this teaching, the images used, it is the sharpness of language, the emphatic vehemence, and the enormity of sexual desire as a sin. Most commentaries on these verses claim Jesus is using hyperbole, exaggeration—and simply emphasizing what was forbidden by the tenth commandment—(Deut. 5:21), "Neither shall you covet your neighbor's wife." Interpreters make allowance for what some of us construe as a crude literalism, and qualify what Jesus said as not a part of the natural, normal desire, which is part of our own human nature, and for whom many temptations come unbidden! The focus he wishes to give is not so much on the idle, lazy, lackadaisical licking of one's lips in envy, as well as lust, as it is upon the intensive, intentional, mental act of targeting the woman for conquest at the expense of all other considerations—"who looks at a women and wants to possess her" (GNB). This, admittedly, is a fatal liability for entering the Kingdom of heaven. I do not think it is helpful for our Lord to have said; "Everyone who looks at a woman with lust . . . has already committed adultery with her."

I say I do not feel this accounting of lust comes through quite this way! It surely may do so occasionally even to the already married. I would guess that most men are not so oversexed that they want to rape every women they see! Feelings range across a wide spectrum of tones, modulations, shadings with every person we encounter.

In addition, as the imagery that follows declares (to our perturbation) the surgical act of amputation, a radical maiming is called an act of violence. Why couldn't Jesus have said something simple like, "Pruning is for the sake of improving the produce of fruit?" The plucking out of the eye and the cutting off the hand I suppose makes sense—our own vehicles of communication. One might casually wonder about the penis, the male organ of sexual intercourse in mammals. In addition, we do not wonder long about this, for that has not been forgotten—as we read in Matthew 19:12, "For there are eunuchs . . . who have made themselves eunuchs, for the sake of the kingdom of heaven." This to me is denigrating, antisex, an affirmation that utterly nullifies God's creation of "male and female." The reference to "eunuchs" is the closest we come to scripture's reluctance to "call a spade a spade"—to refer to genitalia, and the "cutting off" the castrating of the male organ.

In the *New Interpreter's Study Bible*, the commentary on verses 27-30, we read, "Jesus interprets the Decalogue's prohibition of adultery to condemn the predatory behavior and structures of a patriarchal society, to curb male power, and to establish different male-female interaction."[25] This is true, and in order to give the clearest meaning to what Jesus says—in terms of our world today—we must realize he could build upon only from the tradition he inherited. From *The Women's Bible Commentary*, there is a perfunctory, factual statement in a book, which has a section entitled "Christian Approaches to Sexuality" in terms of the attitude that prevailed in the patristic era—the first four, five, centuries of Church history. "There was in general an embarrassment, suspicion, antipathy, and abhorrence with respect to physical sexuality." The "givenness" of our sexuality is probably one of the most important features of our humanity. Such an inclusive condemnatory statement as this should prompt us to challenge its claim and to probe its causes. Those of us who have read some of the theological works of the titans that lived in that time—Jerome, Tertullian, and Augustine—are familiar with their severe denunciations of marriage, precisely for its sexual aspects. The answer does not lie wholly in the Hellenic culture of those days. Some information is disclosed to us as we look more carefully at what the New Testament scriptures say and do not say about how people lived back then. Today we can say that the problem can be attributed to an inadequate anthropology—with reference to the difficulty of actually accepting the distinct sexuality as expressed in "man," "woman," and of accepting the focus given of the interaction that takes place between them!

It could be said that there is no mention in the Gospels, probably the entire New Testament that can be claimed, to give any identity, or warrant, for the fact of human sexuality—in either feelings or allusions that would make it apparent, that is, other than in its sinful manifestations! (Jesus's Sermon on the Mount in Matthew 5:27-30; and the story of "The Woman Caught in Adultery" in John 8). I suppose if we look at the story of Jesus at the home of Simon the Pharisee (Luke 7:36-50), it could be said that our Lord was subject to intimate sensual pleasure (which he does not thwart) expressed by the "sinful" woman emerging into his personal space: "She stood behind him at his feet weeping, and began to bathe his feet with her tears and to dry them with her hair. Then she continued kissing his feet and anointing them with the ointment." The only other time Jesus is given a kiss is from Judas in Gethsemane at the Arrests (Mark 14:45). There might be one other exception to my blanket estimate—when in public a woman spoke up "raising her voice, saying to Jesus: 'Blessed is the womb that that bore you and the breasts that nursed you!'" (Luke 11:27-28). This was intended as a compliment; indirectly too a comment on Jesus's "good looks." But the intent is somewhat lost in Jesus's towering declamation: "Blessed rather are those who hear the word of God and obey it."

Were we to assess the meaning that our own sexuality has for us today, we would find that we are on quite a different "frequency" from that of our forefathers, and assuredly, from whatever "imprints" we can detect that prevailed in biblical times.

I quote, "By collapsing the distinction between thought and action, this extension of the law against adultery to include lust suggests that no one should be regarded as a sex object."[26] The burden here is placed on the man; women are not seen as responsible as enticing men into sexual misadventures." However, we might well add today that in fact they are! In *Preaching through the Christian Year*, Craddock and others argue "that rather than blinding the eyes, one would do better opening the eyes to see and learn more about the person who might be an object of inordinate desire. Lust is usually toward strangers . . . but once these persons have names, families, dreams, plans, fears, and concerns . . . once one knows personally the other—the nature of the attraction is radically altered and takes on a wholeness of which sex is only a part."[27] To know "the other"—consistently, in the measure of some breadth and depth—might well put the brakes on the momentary impulse.

The intractable factor, I think, is the fact that in the Hebrew scheme of things, women were regarded as "property." On this basis, she is already an "object"—lacking in personal identity. The words "covet" and "lust" translates from the same Greek word. The financial investment by a husband in his wife could have dwelt in the sharpness of Jesus's use of this expression—"that everyone who looks at a woman with lust has already committed adultery with her in his heart." This teaching is part of a great block of his discourses (probably from Q) crafted, edited by Matthew, in whose gospel *only* it appears. Accepting as most of us do, the priority of Mark's gospel, we seek to trace it back; where it does not occur, but the penalty for lust does occur, in the penalty for lust as the same—"the cut-off-hand," "the plucked-out eye," but with a different context. In Mark 9:42-48, here Jesus is solicitous about "one of these little ones who believe in me" and the fact that there are such people that could put a "stumbling block" before them at the very beginning of their journey in life. In our contemporary world today, what comes to mind, of course, is the pedophile, the one who has what is truly a most grievous abnormal condition—sexual desire for a child. Fortunately, in the unfolding biblical tradition of the Christian movement, and the church's mission, men do not emerge as dangerous exploiters of women, neither woman as seductresses. We read mostly of women as mothers, sisters, wives, and craftspeople.

We get an interesting answer when we ask Jesus, what is there in the human heart that can make me unclean? Matthew and Mark readily give us the stock answers: "For out of the heart come evil intentions, murder, adultery, fornication, theft, false witness, and slander. These are what defile a person, but (not) to eat with unwashed hands. In Matthew 15:19-20 and in Mark 7:20-21, there is a little more complete list; "It is what comes out of a person that defiles. For it is from within, from the human heart, that evil intentions come; fornication, theft, murder, adultery, avarice, wickedness, deceit, licentiousness, envy, slander, pride and folly." All these come from within, and they defile a person. To translate these into psychological terms, that contained in the contents of each human soul are "feeling" tones, that are both conscious and unconscious, which become "present" in dreams, complexes, that can be chronicled—psychology provides the typology by which we may find our way through the "filaments" of psychic energy at work in the human soul. In 1913 the break between Sigmund Freud and Carl Jung occurred—which struck at the central role Freud had attributed to sexuality. Here I would quote from a paragraph in Wayne G. Robbins's *Jung and the Bible*: "Freud had understood the libido primarily as a manifestation of instinctual drives; hunger, aggression, and sexuality." (He sought a "bulwark against the black tide of mud.") Jung, however, began to see the libido in terms of a more general psychic energy. Comparable to physical energy, which could appear in many forms, sometimes in sexuality there could also be expressed, "creative and constructive achievements in the individual as well as blindly instinctive forms of behavior."[28]

To realize this possibility, we must do justice to what Jesus has to say about the contents of the human heart—to include a broader picture of what resides in it. In the parable of the different kinds of soil, into which the seed (the Word of God) is cast, in Matthew 13, we read, "But as for what was sown on good soil, this is the one who hears the word and understands it, who indeed bears fruit." He recognizes that "every good tree bears good fruit (7:17). When he is asked by the Pharisees about the coming of the Kingdom of God, he declares it is "not coming with things that can be observed, for, in fact, the kingdom of God is among, within, you" (Luke 17:7). St. Paul elaborates on the intimate nearness of God's word that it is "on your lips and in your heart." "One believes with the heart and so is justified" (Rom. 10:8-10). In 2 Corinthians 3, Paul calls his fellow Christians "our letter, written on our hearts, to be known and read by all, a letter of Christ, written not with ink but with the spirit of the living God, not on tables of stone but on tables of the human heart." The most revolutionary part of Jesus's teaching is that a good inner disposition—a good heart—is more important than following codes of conduct for external behavior, and dividing the world into "the clean" and "the unclean." The structure and dynamics of the human soul, as understood by Jung, which can include psychic material from "the collective unconscious" does help "level the playing field" for the possible options of "the soul" in pursuing the course of its destiny through life. However, as best as we can determine, it still appears that Jesus distances himself from the taint of sexual desire. In his early teaching on marriage Mark 10:1-12 reaffirms the tradition of Genesis 1:27-28 and 2:15-25, but with nary a biographical tidbit! Were I to have been present, I would have wanted him to expatiate from his arsenal of wisdom to comment on the Lord God's declaration, "It is not good that the man should be alone; I will make him a helper as his partner" (verse 18). This is an area where we all need help. There is a raft of issues that need addressed when we seek to make a transition from being a single person, to being a married person. We think about, and often know, of all those young people on the threshold of adolescence, who at the least have concerns and are sometimes frightened by all the developments bursting forth in their bodies. "Coming of Age" involves constant disclosure and crosscurrents, unfolding between mind, spirit, body of "gifts" that demand their attention. How are they to celebrate one of the sweetest epochs in their lives as a boy or girl? For some, sexual desire can be a relentless, insistent, overmastering desire. For some young men, it can feel like he is a stallion in need of constant bridling!

We are indebted to Matthew Fox, for his book entitled *Sins of the Spirit, Blessing of the Flesh* for what he has done to make an accurate assessment of the word "lust." There are two sides, two parts, to the definition of this word. It is both good and bad! There is much to be said for its good side; "Without lust, none of us would be here. Our parents' lust is what brought us into this world. Lust in itself, then, is holy . . . sacred desire wanting to penetrate and connect with another . . . Eros is profoundly near, intimate, reciprocal . . . true love is enhanced and reinforced by the sexual act." We learn what "closeness, caring, regard, respect, affection, fondness, tenderness" are all about.

The negative side of lust makes itself known to us, sometimes too close for comfort. We see so many instances where the harvest it reaps is

one or another variation of violence. Then it comes through as neither a
blessing nor a healing wholesome experience. When lust becomes a vehicle
for objectifying, it becomes a force that needs checking! This kind of lust
will commit the most savage of crimes to satisfy itself—as we see in King
David's murder of Bathsheba's husband (2 Sam. 11). Our vocabulary is rich
in names for describing when things get out of balance, abuse, obsession,
debauchery, licentiousness, plundering.[29]

Our Book of Common Prayer makes a similar distinction of meaning
with the word "desire(s)." In the Baptismal Covenant, in the Presentation
and Examination of the Candidates, the question is asked, "Do you
renounce all sinful desires that draw you from the love of God?" The answer
is, "I renounce them." The word is properly qualified in this regard.[30] Not
all desires are sinful!

It is important that we be aware that our minds and hearts are filled
with a variety of desires, which can make the course of our lives difficult.
We have needed to heed the advice of Ecclesiasticus (2) who said, "My
child, when you come to serve the Lord, prepare yourself for testing . . .
Set your heart right and be steadfast, and do not be impetuous in time
of calamity . . ." "Do not winnow in every wind, or follow every path"
(5:9). Much of our living may necessitate our being on the far side of
knowing what things are like first-hand. We may indeed have "an inquiring
and discerning heart" (p. 308, BCP). We need the discernment, not to let
ourselves be driven by curiosity, so that our desire to know vaunts itself
beyond what brings the peace and well being in which our soul can develop
and be at peace.

There is an element in my own makeup that I feel has protected me
from perils, dangers, and mishaps. I don't know what to call it—other than
a sense of *shame*. Each of us needs to fathom our own experience of this
word. If an evil impulse in us desires that which is plainly forbidden, and
we are tempted by it, to seriously contemplate giving in to it, then a host
of consequences loom up in our imaginations. Most of us are old enough
to have seen people acting foolishly in public and in private. The avenues
of sexual liberality have their respective risks. It might seem simple enough
to write a paper on "Falling in Love" as I have done here. Complexities
abound when you begin to consider the sequel "Staying in Love." I have
a memory of when I was eight years old, of an older relative, who had too
much to drink. He frightened me because the alcohol framed him into
becoming a different kind of person. Many of us older men, who served in
the military, can recall those nights in the barracks, even in Basic Training,

when we'd get into a seemingly endless "rap session." There were always one or two, who would go on, regaling us (so they thought) with vivid details of their most recent sexual exploits, conquests! Not in the least being led to, "can you top this." I think what appalled me at the time was how men in their early twenties could even talk about such things!

There seems to be in me a mysterious subjective—more like "a godly motion" than a radiant signal—that gives me a quiet pause preventing me from doing what could be called a shameful act. Each and all of us can recall when this kind of thing occurs—when we are in a somewhat perilous dilemma. There is something that calls me up short from doing something dishonorable, disgraceful, in my person, in front of someone, or to someone. I do not know what else to call it, but "a sense of shame." It forestalls my acquiescence, perhaps because I am better able to envisage its consequences, to think it through. I am not a prude, nor am I overmodest. There is a fastidious streak in me—this could mean I have artistic pretensions. If I become oversensitive, then certain things disgust me. I guess I am just more comfortable in a more orderly world!

Contributions of the Romantic Movement

At this point, I would like to deepen our understanding of romantic love—as a part of our need to see everything that exits in God—"entheos." Is love the true essence of what we might call "the poetry of creation?" Is romantic love more than just a desperate appropriation of nostalgia? Why do personal intimacies matter? Eros has been battered from many quarters these last hundred years—from militant feminism, women's outreach transcending "the glass ceiling" occupationally in all professions, sports, space, government, including the military. We have today sex therapy surrogates, artificial insemination, computer-dating services. In an age engulfed by sexual liberations, is it possible even to believe in romantic love anymore? Is it possible to convert idealizing lust into an ethic for marriage? I propose we can tackle our task by looking briefly at the experiences of people, through the context, principles, and insights, of what is termed "romanticism"—the Romantic Movement in literature and the arts that all began in Europe toward the end of the eighteenth century, flying its colors by emphasizing the imagination and emotions over intellect and reason. It was a reaction away from classical Rome and Greece, seeking to capture what was missing—"something more deeply infused' (Wordsworth).[31.] Its contribution to culture involves a host of aspects that make clear definition nearly impossible. Its main principles are as follows:

(1) Belief in the innate goodness of human beings
(2) Reverence for nature
(3) Flight from the city
(4) (For the English) Retreat to the lake country

(5) Freedom of thought that includes both revolt against political authority and social convention, against the mind that forges manacles of custom and conformity

(6) The exaltation of physical passion and physical activity

(7) A persistent but ambivalent attraction to the supernatural, the morbid, the melancholy, and the cruel—as appearing, for example in the Gothic novel.

We are to note the concurrent time frame of these things in which these tendencies took place with both the French Revolution and the Declaration of Independence by the American States. There is evidence from the social structures of the day in England, that much in society had become an evil force, oppressing and stunting its citizens. The evils of the day included the slave trade, press gangs recruiting seaman for the merchant marine, the demands of industrialization upon children, the poor, enclosures of common public space by the rich, issues of public health, the need for less stringent legal codes. It was as if a dark repressive cloud had cast itself over vast segments of citizenry that both obscured perception and limited action. It was no wonder that the wellspring of the Romantic Movement came as a discovery that beauty, goodness, and justice could still be found in its most natural settings—in the pleasing qualities of landscape!

The religious awakening of the country under the preaching and ministries of John and Charles Wesley did more than launch methodism. It also freed up in the common people emotions, sentiments, and even enthusiasm. Many who might not understand the doctrines still would be touched intuitively to make them credibly their own. That brought forth to them a sense of dignity and self-respect, and prompted a reading of the Bible, which became available from the proliferating printing and publishing business. The subjective poetry of Wordsworth (*The Prelude*) and Coleridge (*Christabel*) led to the habit of introspection, and even to a shift in religious ideas and the pioneering of new tracts of spiritual realities. The guarantee of sense impressions furthered the advance of consciousness. One commentary of this period marks it as a time of "fragmentation" of consciousness. Focus became important upon the mind of human beings, and so led to the contemplation and study of the inner consciousness of people—not just of "class" but also of ordinary people, children, shepherdesses, beggars, and sailors. There occurred the development of the vernacular in language—the conversation of people who are free from the perversions of taste through the fads and fancies of the day, but who still speak from their actual experience of knowledge. For example, many poets extracted from autobiographical material the fact that young people seemed to experience a period of melancholy through which they had to pass. To reminisce about this led to a deeper understanding of the psychological stages human beings went through from childhood to mature adults. Feelings emerging from sense impressions, and the emotions in response to live crises continued as a current over the years. Further feelings would arise, but they did so from ideas undergoing change from the power of association with one another!

Connected with this process, according to Wordworth, were two concepts—fancy and imagination. Fancy was linked with youth, and imagination with maturity! Poetic faith for the romantics usually requires "a willing suspension of disbelief." Coleridge's poem *Christabel* is cast in the shadows of a dream world. Arthur Beatty, [32] in his book *Romantic Poetry of the Early Nineteenth Century,* praises this poem because it sets forth "a love persisting long after estrangement and asserting its power into the most unexpected occasions."

The first figure we are looking at is one who eloquently represents the Romantic Movement (English), Samuel Coleridge Taylor (1772-1834). He was a poet, philosopher, and theologian. Through his respect for the Bible as a document fit for the spiritual needs of people, he became the Father of the Broad Church movement in the Anglican Communion. He represents the protest of Romanticism against the Rationalism of the eighteenth century including a fossilized Protestant orthodoxy! In one sense, he was a "brilliant failure," whose gifts were dissipated in an abstruse speculation, and undermined by addictions. He was not happily married. In addition, he regaled with William Wordsworth (1770-1850) in the shift from satiety with order to the discovery of beauty, goodness, and vigorous expressions that pervade the uncultured world of nature. A contagious fire took place in the hearts of these men, offering a newfound freedom to attune themselves to its wonders by means of their own God-given sensibility, sensitivity, and sentiment. Coleridge provides us with a prototype, a formula, for assessing the dimensions of "romanticism" a measuring rod, which delineate its characteristics, its expressions! He was critical of the empiricism of the day that regarded the mind as simply a tabula rasa,—a blank tablet, an empty receptacle, simply fed by sense experience. He focused intently on "the shaping spirit of the imagination." In chapter 13 of his *Biographia Literaria*, he divides the imagination into two—the primary and secondary. The primary imagination is the first act of self-consciousness, which makes knowledge and perception possible. It is a "repetition in the finite mind of the eternal act of creation in the infinite I AM." This declaration unites the perceiver and the perceived in one act. The secondary part is the poetic imagination, which brings that fusion of perceiving mind and perceived object out into the world. This poetic aspect involves "deep feeling and profound thought—what we call "insight," which interprets, shapes, and recreates original experiences. This vitalistic concept of the human mind as having power to impose form, order, and spirit upon sense experience, repeating as it does so, repeats the eternal act of creation in the infinite declaration I AM. Its promise is the capacity to bring forth new worlds.

Pertinent to our concern is the explanation Coleridge gives to the symbol-making faculty of human imagination. It works with the tools of myth, metaphor, analogy, parable, allegory. It is the reciprocity between the mind and what it perceives, when stored in our memories, that gives new life to us in times of sadness, depression, adversity. The human mind deals most adequately with reality by this "mode." That is to say, the human mind works not primarily in terms of rigid, logical, rational analysis and argument, but in terms of its symbol-making power. The symbol does not contain the whole of the idea. However, the symbol is not just suggestive, but constitutive, and does partake of the reality it represents. It has power to open up the reality of the outer world, but also unlocks the hidden and unknown consistency of the human soul, evoking and eliciting the response of the whole person. An example might well be to recall your memory of the most beautiful landscape or seascape you have ever seen! It is by the imagination working in and through the symbols, signs presented to itself that the whole world comes into being. In learning something about the beauty of a rose, one learns something about the beauty of one's beloved. In learning about the love of a man for a woman, one learns something new about the phrase "God is love" (1 John 4:8). George MacDonald (1824-1905),[33] Scottish poet and novelist once said, "There is not a form that lives in the world, but is a window cloven through the blank dark of nothingness, to let us look into the heart, feeling, and nature of God." Sometimes, like a snowball rolling downhill, the symbol may take unto itself everything it meets along the way, wrapping into its own unity even discordant, contrary, and qualities. Symbol-making is a religious act with its own specific spiritual identities. Coleridge insists "words" are prime symbols and have the same significance as any visible symbol such as a picture. He preached and championed the cause of poetic expression, and said that we need to have a deep and abiding trust in language, taking our cues from the

Holy Scriptures, which he called "the living educts of the imagination." A new and strange term he used to describe the state we are in when we move beyond simply "fixing" ourselves on an "object" of love—to which we are drawn. He says that one experiences "translucence"—love shining through as a gleaming light when one's love is contained in a mysterious web. In this mystery, things work as a magnet, weaving together the invisible strands of two people in love with one another.

William Blake (1757-1827) was an engraver, painter, poet, and mystic. The figure of the young chimney sweeper is dear to Blake, especially in his perilous tasks of removing soot from the chimneys as we remember in *Mary Poppins*. In the context of the religious dimensions of his day, he was antinomian—an attitude of mind that favors grace-faith over law. He personally felt and experienced the harshest and binding cultural confinements of the century![34] If as the rationalist John Locke had declared the human mind to be a "closet," then for Blake it was also a prison cell.[35] If the human body was to be regarded as a containing power, for Blake it was also a source of vehement, impetuous energy that refuses to be bound by the demands of convention. He refused to have any truck with guild-ridden religious teachings. As he looked out on his world, he saw human beings shackled, fettered, haunted by the image of imprisonment, people confined in gloomy, restrictive, places (including invisible "chains"), fearful of the future. He saw all this even as he walked the streets (and ghettos) of London. He echoes Jean Jacques Rousseau, who said, "Man is born free, and everywhere he is in chains."

Part of his failure in his craft may be attributed to the fact that he did not take easily to the custom of "patronage." He once saw "a tree full of angels." In the piece entitled "The Marriage of Heaven and Hell," he gives us proverbs that seek to establish union between reason and energy. Here are packed together some of his most explosive maxims. He was an insistent believer in the sanctity of human passion as in "the soul of sweet delight can never be defiled." He inveighed against systems that support reason at the expense of imagination. He celebrated the physical life in which we partake as the prime manifestation of divine abundance. If "the pride of the peacock is the glory of God," then "the nakedness of woman is the work of God." The beauty of a beautiful woman includes "infinite excellencies that even elude a lover." I really wonder why it took so long for someone to say this kind of thing. One of my favorite sayings of his is, "Eternity is in love with the productions of time." Blake's criticism of Christian moralists is that they are always seeking to make arbitrary distinctions between body and soul, good and evil. He is right when he says, "man has not body (or body parts) distinct from his soul." Our bodies are "contained" by the complete presence of our souls.

He points to the sifting, sorting, changing of scenarios that goes on in the lives of people as they interact with one another and their world. He presents a tableau in which there are two scenes. The first is one in which there is a human being undergoing and initiating strong physical action, but also responding to stimulating external influences—challenges by which he is enveloped, such as in a game or dance contest, or as in a time of sexual love when sensory affection is both bestowed and reciprocated. The second scene would be one that diffuses a feeling of utter tranquility in which a person is quiescent, passive, wrapped in deep thought, responding to the inner illumination of some great vision, with ecstatic sequences of contemplated truth emerging. In both scenes, the exercise of energy is being expressed. Here is a radical alteration of mood and mode, action, background, light and sound, yet both express the truth of the human soul.

The Bronte family—on the eve of the three sisters becoming publishing successes (in a man's world) consisted of the father, Patrick (1771-1861), Branwell (sadly, a lush) (1817-1848), Charlotte (1816-1855), Emily (1818-1848), and Anne (1820-1848). Their mother, Maria, died at age thirty-eight in 1821. All lived in the country rectory at Haworth in Yorkshire—cramped parsonage—seemingly suffocated by small rooms. They lived in a fantasy world, feeding off each other's active imaginations—creating stories close to the circumstances of their own lives. The wild moor with its turbulent weather provided appropriate settings for the weaving of their own tales as adults. There is an overdue justice to be done to the reputation of their father, Patrick, who for decades was regarded as an irascible, remote, stern cleric. He was not immune, however, to the claims of his own ministry as a Low Church Anglican parson, nor was he insensitive to the shifting social and economic events of his day, such as the Luddites (the Chartist movement)—those who opposed the technological advances, the labor, saving textile machines, which produced mass unemployment. The novels the sisters wrote—such as *Wuthering Heights*, *Jane Eyre*, and *Agnes Grey*—with characters such as Heathcliff, Edward Rochester, the heartless coquette, Rosalee. These people are of interest to us because of the kind of people that are portrayed, for they appear in marked contrast to the apparent quiescent personalities of the authors. We are surprised by how intensely alive the heroes and heroines turn out to be—especially those subject to the phenomenon of "falling in love." Both high levels of courtship and the ratcheting up of emotions are manifested along the sequences of plot!

In a multiple narrative structure, we see emerging strong, compulsive personalities interacting with others of a contrasting nature. There are those living out the destinies of their impulses from a disquieting vision, which never leaves them. They seem driven to reclaim loss, to compensate for neglect—even to the point of including revenge. There are scenes that remind us of the condition faced by the neglected orphan—which we find in the stories of Charles Dickens. Autobiographical "bits" emerge in woman characters who suffer from rigid contractions of contact—extreme conditions of stagnation and loneliness. Eruptions occur when they must confront those whose florid passions are woven together in combination with instinctual pride. We do not see such people as this as they themselves could become—were they to recede into a passive mode or perhaps a forgiving mode to slow down in order to see more objectively what is unfolding in their lives.

Our tribute to the Brontes has to do with the emergence in their stories of what today we would identify as psychological states, aberrations, marked by neurotic, even psychotic symptoms. It would seem to me difficult to be "locked" into a marriage, or even in a sustained love affair, even with its frequent ecstatic moments, with another person, who always seems to have "an axe to grind," or a vendetta to discharge![36]

The next figure we look at is a Church of England cleric—interestingly controversial. He is the Reverend Charles Kingsley (1819-1875). He was a man of many interests and enthusiasms. In addition to his career and calling as a parish priest (as was his father), he was an early environmentalist, a pamphleteer, a social reformer with special focus on public health and the plight of the working classes, and a popular novelist. His *Water Babies*, published in 1863, became one of the juvenile classics in the nineteenth century and brought about passage of the Chimney Sweeps Regulation Act the year after the issue hit the presses. Growing up in a typical Victorian household (with the use of a birch cane for discipline), he was not too close to his father as he was to his mother. The severity of punishment aggravated the personal problem of stuttering, which remained a problem much of his life. When he himself became a father, his son Maurice described home life as "a place of perpetual laughter." Charles was never a Sabbatarian. As a parish priest, he maintained continued contact with the people of his "flock" in their homes. He was never a remote "father" neither in the home, not with his many farm families. He was familiar with the science of hedging, ditching, rotating crops, and he was a good horseman. He was able to get along with the workingman. His sympathy with agricultural laborers and their working conditions is reflected in the novel *Yeast* published in 1848, and in his book *Alton Locke—Tailor and Poet* published 1876, which depicts the savage sufferings undergone by a tailor who deserts his "class" to rise above it. As "the parson," Kingsley offered his own people classes, programs, study groups, a lending library, as well as "bread and soup" at the rectory kitchen on Sunday at noon. Frequently his efforts were extended to someone who simply wanted to read and write.

His other achievements became apparent, as he himself became known in England (as well as America) during his mature years. He was a tutor of History to the Prince of Wales, chaplain to Queen Victoria, preached at Buckingham Palace on a Sunday in 1859, became a Canon at Westminster Abbey and one at Chester Cathedral (1870-1873). With his daughter Rose, he became a popular speaker on a lecture tour that brought him to the United States (1783-1785). During the time of the Chartist Rising (1848)—working class discontent—he plowed "new ground" as being the first clergy person to give voice for their needs for emancipation, and for organizing in order to be represented. His Christian socialism moved more in the direction of education and Public Health (Sanitation) than any radical political change.

What brought public attention to him as an author was the dramatic dialogue he wrote in 1848, published by *Fraser's Magazine*, entitled "The Saint's Tragedy," a biography of Saint Elizabeth of Hungary (thirteenth century), including line drawings by the author. She was the very young wife of Louis IV of Thuringa, who died in the Crusade of 1227. Driven from the Court by his brother, she ended up in Marburg under the spiritual direction of Conrad, papal inquisitor, who took advantage of her desire to do Christian (charitable) good deeds for those in need. As her spiritual director, he was cruel, ruthless, even separating her from her children. His excessive severity with her hastened her death at age twenty-four—for Kingsley, "a victim of monkish torture," Conrad was eventually murdered.

In the contemporary world for Charles Kingsley, he contended with aspects of the Oxford movement, the Anglo-Catholic revival, the Tractarians, when the inheritance of the church as the "Kingdom of Christ" was being reevaluated. He took a stand against what he saw as the ascetical practices of the Roman Catholic Church—their position on celibacy, their having monks and nuns, and such things as the stigmata, the virginity of Mary's mother. He was strongly averse to many forms of asceticism—which set up a polarization between the flesh and the spirit, which in his day and age meant a "latter day return to Manichaeism." He deplored the use of the "hair shirt," iron girdles, flagellation. He also embroiled himself in verbal sparring with John Henry Cardinal Newman, when he declared in 1836, "Truth for its own sake has never been a virtue with the Roman clergy." He felt the "weapons" of the Church are simple enough—prayer, holiness, love—to do its work in the world and accomplish its mission ("for the weapons of our warfare are not merely human, but they have divine power to destroy strongholds"—2 Cor. 10:4). Therefore, it is not necessary to resort to extravagant claims to prove one a Christian believer.

What turned out to reaffirm his position on ascetical practices was something that unfolded itself in his personal life. While still a student at Cambridge University (1838-1842) in the year 1839, when he was twenty years old, he met four sisters—the Misses Grenfells in Oxfordshire—orphans, but not children, for they were in their twenties, thirties. He became fascinated with the youngest, Fanny, who is actually described somewhere as "well-upholstered." He found that she was someone with whom he could express what was upon his heart—unreservedly. Also there stirred in him something that made him feel that he must come to Christianity anew, as he felt repelled by the tepid Christianity of his father. Soon beginning a lonely curacy in Hampshire, he was separated by distance from Fanny, and so they began what became a sustained practice of writing letters to one another. Shortly after Charles's death (1875), Fanny published some of his letters to her but heavily edited. According to Susan Chitty,[37] some three hundred letters have become available, through the generosity of a family member, including letters found in a locked diary kept by Fanny in Nice during the year of separation from Charles in 1843. They reveal a side to his life described as "forbidden depths." This diary contains some of Charles's erotic drawings. The peaks and valleys of his feelings are unleashed in their near-daily communication with each other. On his part, there were moods of bleak despair. He tells how he would wander from one room to another, utterly restless. The letters from him spill over with profusions of affection. In addition, with her, he could open the floodgates of his private fantasies. He professes feeling that he cannot survive without her as his mate. The thought of her body haunted him day and night. His "love life" elicited moments of self-abasement and shame—to which he gave voice. There were constant references as to his looking forward when he could "take her into his arms again." In Lent he fasted, and inflicted upon himself something painful that would "mortify his flesh." They were officially engaged in September 1843 and then were wed in Trinity Church, Bath 1844. It should be said that his letters from Fanny reciprocated effusions of affection similar to his own. It appears that he could only accept carnal relationships with Fanny as his wife once he had convinced himself that the human body was holy, and that the act of sex was a sacrament—in which he was the priest.

Even during their engagement, Charles confesses that Fanny permitted him "exceptional liberties." Reference is made to a "delicious nightery." Within the context of Victorian courtship, it is hard to imagine this kind of a thing was repeated too often! He declares, "I cannot wash off the scent, and every moment the thought comes across to me of those mysterious recesses of beauty where my hands have been wandering, and my heart sinks with a sweet faintness and my blood tingles . . . in calm joy and thankfulness to our loving God." Both felt they were closest to God when they shared their nakedness in each other's presence. This becomes apparent when we examine his erotic drawings, to which we have access in Susan Chitty's biography *The Beast and the Monk*. All through his life, Charles remained enormously attracted physically to his wife, Fanny, even though there were times when she could be "bossy" and unduly concerned about appearances. His love letters make it clear that Charles had a sensuous nature in which inhibitions could still play a part. Given the customs of the day, the letters that can still be tracked down make fascinating reading, yet in some ways bizarre, for they are the kind that might be found today in a magazine like *Cosmopolitan.*

Relevant to our purpose is the fact that one of the renewal movements of the church that surfaced during the last half of the twentieth century is Marriage Encounter, which involves couples brought together for a two—to three-day weekend under a simple structured leadership. The most prominent memory that I recall when Dorothy and I went on one back in the eighties was the fact that we spent a good chunk of the time in our own room writing letters to one another, which was a major part of the agenda. Time was to be given to our writing—responding to both verbally and transcribing our responses on a host of "issues" attached to what we would encounter in a typical day—"the trivial round, the common task." However, all was to be connected with our feelings. No particular opprobrium was to be linked with bad feelings. No particular virtue was to be ascribed to good feelings. Feelings were to be treated as facts, and when expressed gave identity to the emotional state or condition we were in when we actually felt them, thus connecting "I feel" with "I am." This made possible the exploration of what it meant not to feel like "myself." We have times when we feel strangely about ourselves, as well as about other people. Concern about these things need to be laid on the table and shared, even though it may be just one other person—your husband or wife. The benefit comes in the better purchase we are given when we look out upon the world, knowing that the "looking out" comes from "within" rather than our being "outside" trying to "look in."

Because Kingsley allied himself with those strongly averse to all forms of asceticism, such as clerical celibacy, monasticism, he became known as a champion of what was called "muscular Christianity." It is a curious term, which probably meant that one was to embrace a healthy style of life in one's habits and activities in order to better fight the "battles" against "sin, the world, and the devil" (formula used in the imposition of the cross on the forehead of the baptized—1928, BCP). For Kingsley, this also included social effectiveness in the political and economic spheres as well. To use such a term as "muscular Christianity" suggests a need to revisit a verse in John's Gospel—chapter 10, verse 10, where Jesus says, "I came that they (referring to Jesus's own sheep) may have life, and have it *abundantly*." This declaration—given the critical word "abundant" in the commentaries I have read, is overshadowed by the imagery which surrounds it, which gives much detail to the imagery of the figures of Jesus as "the gate" and Jesus as "the Good Shepherd." Not many synonyms are needed here, but they can be mentioned; an ample and overflowing life, which includes capacity, the free and energizing exercise of gifts, talents—all in contrast to what is thin, narrow, feeble, lacking in intensity. This is such a simple declaration, rooted in specific intentionality! It brings us to the point of asking: what is the place of the enjoyment of the created order, with its varied delights, its inviting blandishments, which often envelops us, and sweeps us off our feet? How often we are drawn to factor these vivid moments into the agenda for our lives. In Hebrew thought, the rabbis insist that humans enjoy the fruits of their created existence. Therefore, of course, sexuality is seen as a positive drive, and that without it, no man would build a house, marry a wife, and have children! A reading of the Gospels makes clear that Jesus was both world-affirming and world-renouncing. A curious section in Matthew 11, he reflects upon his own ministry, sensing an ironic twist as to its effectiveness. "But to what will I compare this generation? It is like children sitting in the marketplaces and calling to one another 'We piped the flute for you, and you did not dance; we wailed and you did not mourn.' For John came neither eating or drinking, and they say 'He has a demon'; the Son of man came eating and drinking, and they say, "Look, a glutton and a drunkard, a friend of tax collectors and sinners!' Yet wisdom is vindicated by her deeds." By drawing the comparison between himself and his cousin John, Jesus sees himself as trying to get people to "dance." Another text, which is world-affirming, may be found in Mark 7, when he says to the crowd: "Listen . . . there is nothing outside a person that by going in can defile, but the things that come out of a person are what pollute, defile, make unhallowed, unclean." In verses 14-16, what affects our attitude toward the content and environment of our outer world is found in the human heart and mind. Surely, we are heartened when we read 1 Timothy 4:4: "For everything created by God is good and nothing is to be rejected, provided it is received with thanksgiving; for it is sanctified by God's word and by prayer." We probably remember the world-renouncing aspects of Jesus's teaching because they are so striking in their imagery. Turn to Luke 9:59-60 and 14:26, Matthew 10:34-36. It can be difficult to "process" deliberate *hatefulness*, not just disregard it, into our souls, and make it an operative part of our behavior.

We look at the word "asceticism" and realize that it is a term used to cover all those forms and exercises of discipline, which are found prescribed in most religious writings. The practices of asceticism can involve the renouncing of things that are good and even proper in order to attain greater control, order, and simplicity in life. When we think of the fifteenth century book *Imitation of Christ*, we are pulled into its imagery to embrace the model it sets forth for our own living of the Christian life.[38] However, we soon are faced with the problem as to whether we could live this way in the context of modernity. So much Christian theology over the centuries tends to spin off into a dualistic, Gnostic view of "matter," especially in terms of the human body. The reason for this is that it is not sufficiently grounded in the principle of incarnation as it applies to Christ himself. If the motive for renunciation is based on the tyranny of the Spirit, overcoming matter, the body, which is inherently evil, then we are on the wrong track. Such renunciation is harmful, destructive, for the flesh is treated as a curse, an obstacle, and the goodness of Creation is impugned.

The last author we are to consider in this section on the Romantic Movement is David H. Lawrence (1885-1930).[39] For us he is last but by no means least. He was born in Nottinghamshire, a working-class mining town in central England. His first novel, *Sons and Lovers* reveals important aspects of his own boyhood and adolescence—especially the close relationship he had with his mother. Published in 1913, it was criticized for its graphic description of sexual relations, which became an omen of things to come. Perhaps the most notorious thing about Lawrence was the banning of his subsequent books. In *The Rainbow*, published in 1915, he was prosecuted for its obscene, immoral content. More than one thousand copies of the book were burned. *Lady Chatterley's Lover* was privately printed in Florence, Italy, in 1928—was banned in the United Kingdom, and not published in the United States until thirty years later. His frankness about sex (and the use of four-letter words—of which he was the pioneer) was to keep him in constant trouble with the law for most of his life!

His other bid for notoriety came about with his association with Frieda von Richthoven Weekly, the wife of Lawrence's own school professor, by whom she already had three children. She also was the cousin of the famous WW1 famous aviator, Manfred von Richthoven (the "Red Baron"). She and Lawrence eloped to Italy and Germany in 1912. He describes her as "earthy, elemental, and passionate." Through rough and smooth, they remained together until his death in 1930. The record of his published works includes include poems, essays, literary criticism, as well as novels, and they each and all tell of his cosmopolitan interests and of how the story of his life became so much a center of controversy (as well as of censorship cases). His writing is at times uneven, too verbose; he is quick to attack people and institutions. But even in the brevity of conversational pieces, his prose is marked by an intensity of feeling, great insight, and the visual evocation of events, places, and nature. He knows how to articulate the rawness of intimate experience. He moves us along with his characters—to explore with him—to probe, beyond the proper limits of curiosity, the varied tones of personal relationships. He lets us know of his insistent rebellion against the mores, customs, conventions of the day. Social evils are woven into the plot. Vast corporate entities are headed for the downward slope—especially those spawned by the intense industrialization going on, combined with a corresponding mechanization and the widespread nationalistic impulse toward war! Lawrence deplores, of course, the Victorian repressive morality, its superficiality, and the austerity of what purports to be its religious life. He throws out a question: "What comes to human beings as their most genuine expression of bodily energy?" This is what gives focus to his vision! Sexuality for him was not so much a throwback of humans to their prehistoric origins, but was given as the sacred means by which a man and a woman could connect with the energies of the cosmos. Therefore, the relationship between husband and wife comes through as the central fact of human existence. In addition, Lawrence surmises that the living nucleus of this identity takes its place in the act of sexual union, which can be complex, even difficult, as well as exceedingly ecstatic. Because of this, it must always be regarded as significant, and treated fairly and honestly. Its spiritual dimensions are not to be ignored, especially as they are translated into our apprehension of the first-hand experience of profound beauty, communicating the true mystery of a shared human existence. With one another, "we" are both ravished through being "touched" by sense and sight.

Help from Our Hebraic Roots (as Scripture)

Looking imaginatively beyond love to the fact of marriage, we find it to have one of the most sanctified of traditions in Judaism, stemming from Genesis 1:27—"So God created humankind in his image, in the image of God he created them; male and female he created them." In Genesis 2:7, "Then the Lord God formed man from the dust from the ground, and breathed into his nostrils the breath of life; and the man became a living being." Here man has a lower origin than the parallel in 1:26. For man is not created in the image of God, but from the dust of the earth, but he also has a closer and more intimate relationship with the Creator, who blows the breath of life into him, transforming him so earth bound, into a living being—a psychophysical unity, who depends on God for his very life. The creation of the woman after the man from a part of his body does not need to imply the subordination of woman. The point of verse 24 is that men are to be different from the males of the animal world, who mate and move on to the next partner. Promiscuity is thus a degradation of God's intention. The Edenic ideal is monogamy! A man wishes his wife to be with him always. This is also the existential paradigm by which a man and woman can find love, security, and companionship. Both the rabbinic and prophetic traditions identify various ways by which people may relate or be related to one another. Celibacy was rejected because it indicated two concerns: first, it violated the mandate in Genesis 1:28—"Be fruitful and multiply"; and second, it meant a diminishment of the "image of God" in the world. To quote Rabbi Eckstein in his *How Firm a Foundation*, the rabbi's claim, "An unmarried man is an incomplete person, bereft of joy, blessing, and goodness. An unmarried high priest was not even allowed to officiate in the temple on the Day of Atonement. Sexuality was seen as a potentially positive drive in rabbinic thought, for *without* these desires, "no man would build a house, marry a wife, or have children."[40] It was recognized in Judaism that a good marriage is not easily achieved, and that a truly reciprocal relationship is girded about by respective obligations. Given each sex's equality in terms of their access to God based on such "identity," each one is free to forge his or her own relationship with God. If this is true then no one else can ultimately define us. We each have as human beings a portable spiritual center that cannot be superseded! There are hints, inklings, to be found in John's Gospel—1:49, where Nathaniel calls Jesus "Rabbi," which may not be an accurate title for Jesus. It is to be noted that in first-century Jewish life, a requirement for being a rabbi included that he had to be married. It has always baffled me why the evidence for Jesus having been married is only surmised. We in our day live in the wake of the popularization of scripture—those who have advanced the cause of historical fiction reproduced through the media. I refer of course to Dan Brown's *The Da Vinci Code*, which sets forth the possibility that not only were Jesus of Nazareth and Mary Magdalene married, but that they also had children! Our own Bishop John Shelby Spong in his book *Born of a Woman* has a well-crafted chapter entitled "Suppose Jesus Were Married." For some this may seem strained exegesis of scripture, but not for me. It does have curious attractions in my own imagination. We labor under a deprivation based on not having a thoroughgoing "incarnationalism." How do we know whether Jesus was truly "man"? Bonnell Spencer, in his book *God Who Dares to be Man*, says a foremost criterion should be "whether a truly human person could have thought and acted that way. He had to have all the limitations, not only of humanity in general, but also of the time, place, and world view in which he lived and expressed himself... Physically Jesus was a Palestinian Jew ... His body was subject to all the usual ills ... he knew poverty . . . He had all the natural functions, including sex. As to how that was expressed in his life, we have no information whatever. For a Jew to reach the age of about thirty without being married, a good guess is that Jesus had a wife and lost a wife before beginning his public ministry . . . It is important *not* to think of him as having some kind of a glorified body or a charmed human life." As Hebrews 4:15 puts it, he was "tempted in every way that we are." That would have been required not only for the genuineness of his humanity, but "also for the salvation he was to effect." Then it is that Bonnell Spencer has this pivotal assertion: "The early fathers (of the Church) recognized that what Jesus did not assume he could not redeem."[41]

A Gospel Story

As we preachers seek to do this, various methods of Bible study are available. I could at this point use the African model in which each participant, taking his turn, shares in response "I hear/see . . ." considers how this passage touches his/her life. I thought, however, that I would make the point that I am familiar with the "spiritual exercises" of Ignatius Loyola (1491-1556), founder of the Jesuit religious order. These exercises are a series of meditations and rules. Requiring continuous self-examination, they stake out a rigorous discipline in order to set one's heart on the path of spiritual growth. First and foremost, one must rid one's heart of all worldly distractions, inordinate attachments, and disordered affections. The goal is conformity to the *image* of Christ. The participant here is to focus his mental attention upon a particular place (location) in which the object of contemplation occurs—as though one was actually there—to re imagine a significant moment in the life of Jesus. One is to visualize intensely what happens, what is said, and who says it.[42] As with any encounter we have with another person, much goes through our own minds. Distractions come and go. Some do not go away. We find we need a timeframe to contain a suspended animation of all that we need to take into account. Questions arise, which unless they are dealt with, we find ourselves unable to go forward. Therefore, taking liberties here with a given text, let me suggest what might pass as a similar situation, in a contemporary setting!

As preachers often do in their sermons and authors who write on biblical themes, I now take the liberty to imagine myself present at an event reported by Matthew, chapter 19. As usual, the context is minimal. It occurs at a midpoint in Jesus's public ministry, when he left Galilee and went into the region of Judea, large crowds followed him, and he cured them there. Some Pharisees came to test him and asked, "Is it lawful for a man to divorce his wife for any cause?" His response starts out (to follow

Mark 10:1-12), which is his reassertion of marriage as founded in creation, the making of "male and female" and that they become "one flesh." He says in effect that if God has joined them together, "let no one separate." For Mark, if either of them divorce, in order to marry another, they commit adultery. However, in Matthew, the Pharisees ask a reasonable question. Why did Moses grant a certificate of divorce? Jesus replies, "Because you were so hard-hearted." But he makes room for the one exception, "unchastity," verse 9.

At this point, we hear from the disciples who pose a question, "If such is the case with his wife, is it better not to marry?" Surely this is an honest question, and it is being asked in a crowd which includes the married and unmarried, as well as the disciples who we assume are for the most part married (Mark 1:30; 1 Cor. 9:3-5). Jesus's reply here puts the whole issue of being *un*married in the context of it being a gift, as much as marriage itself.

I try to imagine what my own response to such a question might be were I to be queried by a gathering in the parish, which would be a mix of young and old. I come up with a different thought progression from what we find to have taken place. I sense the question, and it is a question the disciples put to Jesus. Surely, some of those present come in wonderment about whether marriage itself is *worthwhile* or that it is beyond the capabilities of ordinary people. In the dialogue that follows, their consideration is not addressed. What we are given is the declaration about "eunuchs," that "there are those who have been so from birth, those who have been made so by others and those who have made themselves so for the sake of the kingdom of heaven" (verse 12). In one sense, I believe we are shortchanged by this reply. What transpires here is similar to what Jesus does when he is asked other questions. He sees the larger context in which an answer would have more meaning or uses the question to make an assertion about himself. If Jesus uses this question to make an assertion about him, he is simply disclaiming his marriage ability for the sake of the kingdom of heaven. Given the question that was asked, it still leaves many other responses that are not addressed. I thought of a young bystander involved in his first serious love affair. I myself would have responded to his quizzical expression, "Yes, it sure is an exciting thing to be in love. It leads you into experiencing your own life in a way that you did not realize possible. It sure is a tall order to contemplate spending the rest of your life with one woman. However, I daresay it could be of some help for you to read about 'the capable wife' in Proverbs 31. If nothing else it enumerates the various ways in which a good wife assumes responsibility for her actions."

In our own search for "the historical Jesus," it is relevant to be aware of his own use of scripture, the heritage of his own people. He did not possess scrolls, but his own free and flexible quotations usually come through with freshness and aptness that is unmistakable. We note how he must have pondered Deuteronomy, Isaiah, the Psalms, other Prophets, and the historical books. With regard to his own soul, he sought to hear God speaking with *one* voice in a lively contemporary way. Unfortunately, there is little if any reference from "the wisdom" writings, other than the Psalms, of the Old Testament. The story of his presence at the wedding in Cana of Galilee, which we use as the introduction in the Book of Common Prayer, "The Celebration and Blessing of a Marriage," to me, tells little about either Jesus's interest or even concern about the fact of marriage in human life (John 2:3, 4). Neither does John the Baptist's self-identification as "friend of the bridegroom" (John 3:29-30).

The Case of a Bridegroom without a Bride

The use of the word "bridegroom" in the Gospels raises a troublesome issue (more so than the word "husband," or even "male"). In Mark 2:19 (and the same in Matthew 9:15 and Luke 5:34), Jesus says, "You cannot make the wedding guests fast while the bridegroom is with them (can you?)." All this says is that fasting and feasting having their appropriate times in life. The mention that such a bridegroom could then be taken away suggests by implication that Jesus could be referring here to himself. In John 3:29, it is John the Baptist who says, "He who has the bride is the bridegroom. The friend of the bridegroom, who stands and hears him, rejoices greatly at the bridegroom's voice. For this reason my joy has been fulfilled." The use of this image has no connection really in terms of the context in which it appears. All that it says is that another person may rejoice in someone else's happiness. From the brevity of the use of the word "bridegroom" (in just these texts) and the fact that there remains unanswered, the question as to the identity of the "bride," I would regard it as an arbitrary "image," an insufficient analogy with inadequate resemblances. There are so many things that can be said about Jesus—some of which are rooted often in obscure details of his public ministry. However, they still "flesh out" what he was like as well as what he did and said. Images abound! Such as Mother Hen (Luke 13:35), Teller of Parables (Matt. 13:3), Quencher of the Thirsty (John 4:7-15; 7:37-39), Trail Blazer for Those in Darkness (John 8:12), Healer of the Sick (Mark 1:32-34), the Good Shepherd (John 10:11-18). However, the Gospels are rather clear about the fact that he never married, nor is there any evidence that he entered into any precondition that would suggest this as a possibility. The singularity of the marriage relationship (which Jesus himself ratified in Mark 10:1-9) does not emerge in whatever kind of radarscope we might use in treating NT data given us.

This fact affects the way we may understand the counsels about marriage given in other parts of the New Testament—the Household Codes in Ephesians 5:22, 1 Corinthians 7, and Colossians 5:18. In the Ephesians passage, we read, "Wives, be subject to your husbands as you are to the Lord. For the husband is the head of the wife just as Christ is head of the church, the body of which he is the Savior . . . Husbands, love your wives, just as Christ loved the church and gave himself up for her, in order to make her holy by cleansing her with the washing of water by the word . . ." To use the relationship of Christ with his church as the basis for an analogy between husband and wife cannot be sustained. The counsel in verse 21 is worthy of being embraced if it is truly believed: "Be subject to one another out of reverence for Christ." Here is staked out an attitude and policy of mutual reciprocity! However, the author who penned the subsequent verses (22-33) does not seem to understand the limits of language. Some of this has to do with the fact that human beings cannot and do not live up to what is set forth as a divine standard. Husbands do not die for their wives as Christ did for the church. The critical condition which lies in the role of the intermediary—in the husband's role—what is crucial may not be that he lacks the ingredient of being "self-loving," but that he is not "self-giving." Things do not bode well for following the course of this exegesis, for through it persists the ingrained, conventional patriarchal practices of that day!

I would call attention to a particular phrase in the prayer book service in the opening paragraph that has endeared itself to Anglicans for centuries. It follows the reference to "the bond and covenant of marriage established by God in creation." Then we read how "our Lord Jesus Christ *adorned* this manner of life by his presence and first miracle at a wedding in Cana of Galilee" (page 423). Granted that the word "adorn" can mean "fitted out," which would be appropriate here, as would "to add beauty, splendor, distinction" to its character set forth in Creation. However, it does not say enough if we were to think that a part of the intention behind the use of the word includes something that would be decorative, like an accessory, an embellishment, the addition of a showy thing. Surely, marriage is meant to be more than this. What would be our basis for considering the word "adorn" to be a weak word here, considering it to reflect in some real measure "the mind of Christ"? I cannot think of what a stronger word would be, which would stake out the fact of marriage in a more positive way. But the need for one remains!

I have a Book of Common Prayer, published in 1727, *Liturgy of the Church of England* with its rites and ceremonies, published in London, England. Following the opening greeting: "Dearly beloved," there are literary selections that have long since been excised. Marriage is not to be enter prized, nor taken in hand unadvisedly, lightly, or wantonly, to satisfy men's carnal lusts and appetites like brute beasts . . . but reverently . . ." In listing the purposes of marriage, the first (back then) of course was "the procreation of children." The second is described as "ordained as a remedy against sin, and to avoid fornication, that such persons have not the gift of continence, might marry, and keep themselves undefiled members of Christ's body." This is a concession originating with St. Paul, who in 1 Corinthians 7:8, 9 counsels "the unmarried and the widows" to remain unmarried"—"but if they are not practicing self control, they should marry. For it is better to marry than to be aflame with passion." It is the negative bias and bent in these references that disturbs me and which leads us to reestablish the positive values and merits of what marriage is really all about—engaging in its appropriate activities, joyfully, without fear, shame, or guilt.

I think I understand as well as most preachers that there are doctrinal reasons why the New Testament does not reflect the reality of human sexuality in a good light. Indeed, taking into account both Jewish and Christian traditions, one could set forth the case that the whole idea of sexual pleasure is to be treated as a concession to our "animal nature" and is thereby less than human. We surely resonate with St. Paul when he says in 1 Corinthians 12:23 that "those members of the body that we think less honorable we clothe with greater honor." Shame is a good thing, but there are times when we cannot relegate our own sexuality to oblivion and pretend it does not exist. The special day in the Christian year known as the Feast of the Annunciation on March 25 commemorates how God made known to the youthful Mary that she was to be the mother of Jesus. I never know quite how to observe this feast, given the supernatural terminology of the Collect, which refers that just by such angelic tidings, we "may by his cross and passion, be brought to the glory of his resurrection." For those of us married folks, there are many other thoughts that cluster around the critical event of our wives experiencing motherhood—for the first time. A birth is always a sequence to a previous condition, based upon the occasion of our engaging in sexual intercourse at a particular moment in time. However, here in this prayer book rite, that core experience is swallowed up in the sanctity of meaning that is imposed upon individuals which really tends to obviate it being connected in any way to their physical satisfaction. There may be something wrong with the way I understand things, but here in the infrastructure of my faith, I find a disconnect!

The Founders of Other Religions

We might wonder about the founder of other religions, as to what extent courtship and marriage might have figured significantly in their life story. Buddhism begins with the life of Siddhartha Gautama (563-483 BC), born into a royal family in the foothills of the Himalayas. He is also called Shakyamuni. He was raised cloistered and in luxury. As to his marriage at a huge athletic competition, he won the hand of a beautiful maiden, Yashodara (keeper of radiance), who became his bride. He was sixteen years old. He is reported to have gotten along with everyone and proved to be a good companion and loving husband. A child was born and named Rahula. However, a crucial stage of his spiritual development took place when he was twenty-nine, when an excursion beyond the palace brought to his attention the facts of aging, disease, and death. It brought about his leaving his wife, walking away from his responsibilities as a father and prince. He severed ties with his hereditary caste and set out as a wandering ascetic in search of enlightenment. He went through many difficult times and survived many evil temptations. By age thirty-six, he came to see the eternal truths he had been seeking.[43]

Muhammad, "the Praised One," also called Mohammed, was the founder of Islam. He was born in Mecca (AD 570-632) and raised by his uncle. When he was twenty-four he married Khadijah, his first of many wives; he was a wealthy man. At forty, he felt the call to be the true prophet of God to the Arab people. Becoming unpopular in Mecca, he fled to Medina (the Hegira) because he claimed to be the last of the prophets; he incurred the displeasure of both Christians and Jews. As to his marital life, he had many wives, a large harem. The nature of desert living brought polygamy to be an economic and cultural benefit. Islam turned out to be a religion of social justice as echoed in the Koran. Karen Armstrong, in her biography of Muhammad, provides us with the latest scholarship about the prophet's wives, Hafsa, Sawdah, and Aisha. They were not always chosen for their sexual charms; some after his death continued to be of a significant influence. The prophet had a tremendous respect for women. No less than 174 traditions counsels were said to have been given to Aisha directly by the prophet himself. Islam did not crush women, as people tend to imagine in the West. Some found that it enabled them to fulfill a potential that would have been inconceivable in "the days of ignorance" (before the Prophet's teaching took hold).[44]

The Holy Spirit

A fortunate addendum is provided to mold the kind of historical development and expansion of some kind of the scriptural imprint in the faith of our lives. The verse of John 16:12 has always exhibited a fascination for me because of the way it triggers my imagination. In staking out a theology of the Holy Spirit, it wisely provides for substantive prospects for the future which may barely exist in any context of a "now" situation. It is in this verse that Jesus says, "I still have many things to say to you, but you cannot bear them now." This "Spirit of truth" will declare to you "the things that are to come." The Amplified New Testament elaborates on the phrase after the word "*but*, you are not able to bear them nor take them upon you nor to grasp them now." In the New English Bible, we read, "But the burden would be too great for you now." We are not to lose the focus on what is being talked about, which is a revelation of the truth of God. So much hinges upon the meaning of the word "bear." Certainly the word implies "putting up with something" (*Webster's Dictionary*) something that may annoy, distress, but not suggesting exactly the way by which one sustains the imposition! To endure something means that something becomes a strain to be tolerated as one moves forward into the future. This has much to do with our own thought patterns about which we were once comfortable with because they seemed so normal. Examples: How many decades did it take for us moderns to really believe that cigarette smoking was truly addictive and extremely dangerous to our health or that there could be such a thing as women priests and that they could be as intellectually and spiritually competent as men in preaching the Gospel and living prototypes of the Christian life?

For the Christian this one verse, "I still have many things to say to you," equips us with a profound promise of flexibility in our personal relationship with the historical Jesus in reference to his own public ministry to us through the Gospel.

Padre Blazon in Robertson Davies's *Fifth Business* muses as he contemplates the Second Coming of Christ, "My own idea is that when he comes again, it will be to continue his ministry as an old man. I am an old man and my life has been spent as a soldier of Christ, and I tell you that the older I grow the less Christ's teachings say to me. I am sometimes very conscious that I am following the path of a leader who died when he was less than half as old as I am now. I see and feel things He never saw or felt. I know things He seems never to have known. Everybody wants a Christ for himself and those who think like him. Very well, am I at fault for wanting a Christ who will show me how to be an old man? All Christ's teachings are put forth with the dogmatism, the certainty, the strength of youth: I need something that takes account of the accretion of experience, the sense of paradox and ambiguity that comes with years! I think after forty we should recognize Christ politely but turn for our comfort and guidance to God the Father, who knows the good and evil of life, and to the Holy Ghost, who possess wisdom beyond that of the incarnated Christ. After all, we worship a Trinity, of which Christ is but one person. I think when He comes again it will be to declare the unity of the life of the flesh and the life of the spirit. Then perhaps we shall make sense of this life of marvels, cruel circumstances, obscenities, and commonplaces. Who can tell? We might even make it bearable for everybody."[45]

Here we see that we need to sift through and identify those points of attraction and disenchantment, those moments of adoration as well as occasions when we are less than responsive to a personal relationship with the Lord Jesus. We need to understand the varying contexts in which we are able to forge clear linkages, with God through the window that opens up beyond the historical Jesus himself as we catch glimpses into his great life in the Trinity as well as into our own.

The Holy Spirit—to believe in its reality as providing us with what is needed to face the agenda of our day—is almost too much of an exciting thing. In the Creed, we say that the Holy Spirit is the Lord, the giver of life. The Word here is singular. Nevertheless, it almost eludes description, for there is no vantage point for us to describe it, him, her—save in the relationship the Holy Spirit has to Christ. There is no physical or material setting, parameter, edge, or texture, where terms of inclusion, exclusion, plus, or minus could apply. What we are left with is to discern the Holy

Spirit as that spiritual presence which connects, holds together, and unifies all things—weaving together and sustaining all the material entities of life in the universe—so that they bear in some mysterious way—some lesser, some more—the imprint of the presence of God.

There is an interesting qualification set forth in Matthew's Gospel, which sets forth the needed provision for everyone of us concerning "the forgiveness of sins" in terms of a separate context. In chapter 12, verses 31 and 32, we read, "Therefore I tell you, people will be forgiven for every sin and blasphemy, but blasphemy against the Spirit will not be forgiven. Whoever speaks a word against the Son of Man will be forgiven, but whoever speaks against the Holy Spirit will not be forgiven, either in this age or in the age to come." The juxtaposition of these two statements is important! In the first, we can visualize ourselves in the presence of the Lord, who is teaching us by talking directly to us! Even the simplest believer would want to assume he is listening to a messenger of God, whose truth is to be received and recognized by him. Moreover, such a person would want to respond with the fullest concurrence that would be possible for him to give. It would emerge from the depths in his own heart whereby he wholeheartedly loves what is good and hates what is evil. Unfortunately, to probe the interaction that goes on in any kind of dialogue that has a conversational caste to it, a whole range of thoughts well up, overtones, undertones, that moves along the spectrum of desire for greater understanding. This makes the transition of one thought from one person to another somewhat complicated to say the least. Even a cursory reading of the Gospels brings us to acknowledge there are "hard sayings," sayings that are even harsh and obscure, sayings that contain textual discrepancies in correlated passages. Even the beatitudes (Matt. 5-7) are difficult to "translate" into a world where the pace is to the swift and the battle to the strong! It is not easy to begin mounting reservations galore when Jesus says in Matthew 8:22 or Luke 60, "Follow me, and let the dead buy their own dead." Why was the fig tree cursed in Mark 12-22, when it was not the season for figs? There is much in the Bible to make us aware of our distance from first-century Judaism. However, we can only offer our adherence to what Jesus says if we can understand the meanings of what he teaches. That is why the commentaries are so important. We probably fall far short of what he expects of us. We have good reason to attend to the other, slightly different "court of appeal" in Matthew 12:32: "Whoever speaks against the *Holy Spirit* will not be forgiven, either in this age or in the age to come."

Revisiting the Gods and Goddesses of Ancient Greece (and Rome)

The polytheism here was different in its religious aspect from that of Judaism and Christianity. It was not a message of salvation, a dogma, or an absolute faith. The Greeks gave us the word "myth" in its double sense. It could mean an archetypal reality, symbolizing certain lineaments of actual life, or it could be a made-up story. The raw material of a myth could be like that of a dream, a fairy tale, or something rooted in legend or folklore. The author Frederick Buechner clarifies this distinction, "A dream may be something that actually happened once upon a time. But myths generally do not tell us much about that kind of actuality. The creation of Adam and Eve, the Tower of Babel . . . in Genesis, do not tell us primarily about events. They tell us about ourselves. In popular usage, a myth has come to mean a story that is not true. Historically speaking, that may well be so. Humanly speaking, a myth is a story that is always true."[46] Myths fix themselves in the memories of a people because they tell us that life is actually more marvelous than it appears—on the surface of things.

A great throng of personages can move through the human memory, because they become products of the way our minds "evolve" them. The great myths are not so much stories invented about people; they are rather "objectifications" of images that lie deep in the human spirit. We get to understand what we are talking about when we understand the difference between the word "character" and the word "caricature." The former is a distinctive mark of identity, an essential quality, position, reputation. The second is a picture or imitation of a person, or thing, a representation, or performance, in which certain features, mannerisms, etc., are exaggerated or distorted, that affect the way you see what you behold, gathering it up in a new essence of being. This can move in the direction of what is bad or what is good. There can be "types" like Witches, Wizards, Ogres, the Wise Old Woman, Earth Mothers, Dragon Slayers, Explorers, Sagacious Animals, and Beautiful Sleeping Princesses. Too often, we go through life, treading old paths, taking the daily routines and people encounters "for granted." We do not see each other in the depth of each other's soul and are never fully aware of the pattern our life has been weaving. There is an "embodiment" of character types that takes place over time, and it recurs in our individual lives and in history—and that is what constitutes "myth." To engage in mythical thinking equips one not only to experience life, but also to possess life with a more adequate grasp. To live in terms of the myth of one's own life means that you are open to an abundant potential that can carry you forward into your future. In terms of the goddesses and gods of ancient Greece, they are not to be worshipped as companions of God in a Christian world and thus mistakenly become subject to the sin of idolatry. Rather they are to be interpreted psychologically, and accommodated, in terms of the movements of what Carl Jung calls "the collective unconscious." Jung probed new terrain, pioneered new advances, which he called "the collective unconscious"—which he identified as a level of the mind, where the source of "archetypes" (ideas) lies connected to images, which surface as forms of behavior.[47] These archetypes can color and give texture to not only my own ego's projection upon others, but also their particular ego's projection upon me.

We might ask, what might we need to bring to the table as a part of our appreciation for this polytheism that includes "pagan" archetypes, which may indeed represent conscious, and unconscious, situations in our own lives? There is no void here in terms of subject matter, but a web of fabulous personages, who are much more than values personified, or "straw" allegorical men and women. Here are almost too-human figures, with various mixtures of frailties, stumbling from one crisis to another in tempest-tossed worlds. These mythic figures do not see themselves as "heroes" or "heroines" by a long shot. But they cast a sufficient presence to generate movements of consciousness in ourselves. We see them caught up in the same conflicts, interdependencies, and participations in both the profane and the sacred—just the way we are! The balance between the male and female, the masculine and feminine, the patriarchal and matriarchal, is never short-changed—in the exploration of imagined worlds, including not a few reciprocal seductions. In addition, there are "real" people who inhabit that narrow band of the human life cycle between childhood and the age of marriage, about which we have a special concern. Before introducing

Venus here (her moment of birth) appears on a shell that serves as a platform. She stands demurely covering her nude body with elegant hands and masses of golden hair swept up by a gentle breeze. Draperies flutter as well as pink rose blossoms. Venus is flanked on the left by the wind god Zephyrus and his companion. The figure on the right is identified as one of the hours, The Horae or Seasons.

the one person who provides some data in our pursuit, I think it only fair for us to list the "tools" by which we may understand the connections, the interplay, the meaning of the context in which so much is held together. I speak of those nine Muses—the nine goddesses who preside over literature, the arts, and the sciences. Calliope is the one with a beautiful voice; her attribute is that of eloquence in reciting epic poetry. Clio is the muse of history. Euterpe charms us with the music of lyric poetry, as Melpomene does with tragedy. Terpsichore delights in dancing. Erato fascinates us with erotic lyric poetry, Polyhymnia with the music of sacred poetry. Urania is the muse of astronomy, and Thalia is the muse of comedy and pastoral poetry.

When we turn to the pantheon of Greek "gods and goddesses," we are presented with a host of people who are daunting even in the pronunciation of their individual names. Aphrodite is the Greek goddess of love, beauty, fertility, and the affections that sustain social life. The origins of her name go back to the word "foam." When the Titan Cronos cut off the penis of his father Ouranos, he cast this member of the body into the sea, where it floated amid white foam. Inside the penis Aphrodite grew and was washed up at Paphos on Cyprus. There were sanctuaries dedicated to her on islands in the east end of the Mediterranean. Botticelli's picture—*Birth of Venus* painted in 1482—commemorates Aphrodite rising on the waves from a seashell. Among the ancient Greeks in their mythology, she was married to the crippled smith god Hephaistos, but she was not faithful to him. She bore children by several other gods, including Dionysus, the god of vegetation, wine, and ecstasy, and the war god Ares, and the dying and rising god Adonis. Because of her unruly behavior, she fell in love with Anchises, the father of Aeneas—a great Trojan hero. She helped to cause the Trojan War by promising Paris, son of Priam, the king of Troy, the hand of the most beautiful woman in the world, which fatefully turns out to be Helen, wife of Menelaus, king of Troy.

Aphrodite's name also has links with the large silver spotted butterfly. The poet Maria Eugenia Baz Ferreira pays tribute to some curious features or traits, characteristics of Aphrodite, when she says, "To all that is brief and fragile, superficial, unstable . . . to all that is light, fleeting, changing, finite, To smoke signals, wand roses, to sea foam, and mists of oblivion . . . to all that is light in weight . . . somber, raving, with transitory words and vaporous bubbly wines I toast in breakable glasses."[48] Yes, Aphrodite cultivates ephemeral beauties—embroidery, flower arrangements, adornments that include perfumes, jewelry—all to make possible encounters to be bathed in a honeyed radiance and shimmering attire. Her poetic presence is assured in all that is graceful, alluring. In those influences at her disposal, she seeks out all living creatures receptive to her desire. Kissing the earth with morning dew, she draws forth from all the hidden promise that love begets life. She gives us courage to probe the wonder we have as to why as created human beings, we reproduce in pairs. She indeed represents this preference for "pairs" and for all the dualisms related to reproduction of our species—the male who stakes out the adventure of seeking a partner, the signals the female and male give to each other; she revitalizes the tensions as well as the magnetic appeal that encourages their union—even within the ebb and flow of the energies when the polarities of sunrise and sunset meet each day.

The qualities of Aphrodite emerge for the most part within those interstices of living that make everyday life more civilized, more beautiful, harmonious. The goddess of flowers suggests refinements of voluptuous delays, artistic nuances. The contrast can be made where the example and presence of Aphrodite prevails and where it does not.[49] Religions that exclude the feminine principle turn sexual energy into a sadistic, oppressive, violent force. There is that harsh, pathogenic, character of an ugly environment, where little more is attached even to the exercise of one's sexuality than that which is dull, mechanical, and hygienic. No effort to be "charming" with and before others is made. Everything that is sensitive, gracious, fragile, is constantly being broken, tarnished, or ridiculed. Even the fetching ways of little children are scrapped. Hunting down evil spirits, demonic hell-raisers, has had such a prominent place in church history that the quest for a connected spiritual life, girded by a living mysticism, has been lost in the shuffle. In the Christian dispensation, there are few, if any examples, of operational integration of body, soul, and mind. The fault may lie in the theology we inherit from scripture. For what is it that we are actually given? Too many features suggest that we are given a monotheistic God as Spirit without a "full" body. It is true that "the Son" lowered himself to our level and deigned to become incarnate, but he is neither a lover nor a father, his mother is still a "virgin," "and his terrestrial life has been presented in a way that could hardly be more disincarnate!" (*Pagan Meditations,* page 44). There is something to be said for this criticism, and it has bothered me for some time now, as a purveyor of the ethical tenets of the Christian religion. The life and ministry of Joseph, the (step) father of Jesus, is of course the appropriate model for all men who follow the Roman Catholic conjugal ethic. There is not even the slightest reference in the Gospel of his personal, intimate, love for Mary that would help young married couples in ascertaining the validity of their own sexual life together.

Aphrodite leaves us with no doubt about her approbation of corporeal realities! She is much "up front" with her "lovely backside," her love of "copulation," "genitals." Modesty has its place, and Aphrodite does have an attraction for veils—the more flattering the better—which both cover and reveal. But there is a time and place for the body's vigorous expression. Her mysterious presence gathers up the whole body—not just the eyes—to know how to breathe, vibrate, resonate, "limb upon limb."

To discover or rediscover the meaning of Aphrodite, we must take into account the poems and songs of Sappho, a historical person, who came to represent a turning point in the history of women's consciousness. She indeed incarnates the goddess's fundamental trait—deeply felt emotion throbbing in the heart that combines a wildness of expression with sophistication, and a taste for adventure, unfolding with an audacity without precedent. Surely, for women as for men, sexual encounter is the most profound human experience. If it is not at least this, the experience makes possible all other relationships. However, now (sixth century BC) it became not only a source of joy and delight, but also the path to each woman's inner knowledge—so that all woman in the wake of such a fact "become priestesses" as to how this insight is to be used! It can take courage on different occasions to yield to sexual desire. This can still include the longing for a child—which arises out of sexual love. The Christian religion in its documents because of its lack of our concern here does not differentiate between a woman's femininity, a woman's marriage, and a woman's maternity. Aphrodite assures the reciprocal pleasure of spouses, which links them together "in the beauty of holiness." Marriage is Hera's domain. We can be captivated by the magic of garments, manifesting Aphrodite, in the flowing together of nature and culture, in a ribbon, a girdle, a bodice, a band of fabric wrapped around the body. Should she be disrobed? The best is to see her half-dressed! The artfulness of women in the realm of seduction has always been and still is the bane, the perniciousness, of patriarchal sensibilities. Yes, Aphrodite wants to play, to dazzle, and to seduce. Sometimes she can be a hot-tempered divinity. There is a generosity of the body that runs as a current through her person—without which there would be neither sexual fusion nor assertive amorous combat—in which each partner contends to be the stronger. Women have less fear of love than men—so that on these grounds alone, a woman can teach a man what he really needs to know, even the factoring in of tears and pain.

The Graces were the three goddesses of joy, beauty, charm, happiness, and feasts. Hesiod gave them the names of Thalia (Good Cheer), Euphrosyne (Mirth), and Aglaia (Splendor). Aside from representing beauty and charm, they were also thought to represent the personifications of overall joy and well-being. They also danced with the Muses to Apollo's playing, as well as be messengers for Aphrodite and Eros.

We now turn to Sappho, a native of the isle of Lesbos (capital Mytilene), a figure of legend as well as of history, whose life span is from 630 to 570 BCE. Ancients and moderns praise her poems, of which only 10 percent have been retrieved—the other 90 percent mostly destroyed by the puritanical efforts of militant churchmen. Literary ancients and moderns claim her poems, which were mostly sung, to be arrestingly incantatory, admirable in their enchantment. She wrote from her subjective personal feelings—her lyrics of love contain many hues of emotion with overtones of great desire, longing, loss, and moments accurately tabulated of infatuation, jealousy, being utterly smitten, and completely fulfilled. Sappho has the woman's eye for "the gorgeous!" Her work shows an interest in the mythic affairs of goddesses with mortals—Aphrodite, Hera, the Muses, and the Graces.

In terms of background, she belonged to an aristocratic family and had access to luxury items and educational resources. Her brother Charaxus held a government post and exported wine. Her reputation, as well as notoriety, is based upon her socially sanctioned "finishing school" for adolescent girls, portrayed as a rather idealized life in those relationships between puberty (childhood) and marriage. Sappho sought to elicit the ripening heart of young girls—dedicated to serving the Muses through games, dances, and songs. This is the setting for most of what she authored. Explicit are moments "quivering with the rapture of complete and harmonious friendship" as they appear in "the ardor and nobility of the feminine soul." This involved a voluntary grouping, specifically designated by gender, but could still express inclusiveness between two women, but also the love between a man and a woman, and also the love between a mother and child. Sappho's lesbianism does not appear to be a refusal of men, but rather a way of refusing to suppress any one sexual preference. In one of her poems, she reports that she had a daughter by the name of Kleis. In 15 BCE, the poet Ovid presents Sappho as a reborn heterosexual, whose previous affections do not compare with her love for Phaon—an Adonis-like figure, the most evident among her (many) lovers. Sappho advises in gnomic, proverbial wisdom. In her day, we would most likely meet with her group—as they would appear as a trained chorus to perform "epithalamia"—wedding songs accompanied by flute and lyre. Their itinerary could include monadic songs—used as a vehicle to share group values (and ridicule those who lacked them). As Sappho's songs "play" with themes of courtship and marriage, they do not have sharp edges nor sneer at others. She exercises unusual objectivity toward whatever the condition of her soul. She even reports to her audience—activating different perspectives within the same poem. She does not get "stretched out" even given her own intense subjectivity. Given her reluctance to impose her own willpower, she does seek to elicit reciprocal response from the other with whom she is involved—so that we have on hand a double consciousness. Emerging here are female characters that are able to live in an autonomous way. Sappho "gives a fully human voice to female desire for the first time in western literature."

Sappho probes the difference between "willed love" and "felt love." If the beautiful includes the intimate, what is it? In a landscape that is "Aphrodisiac," a lush vivid picture of a gardenlike sanctuary turns out to be a repeated metaphor for a woman's sexuality, where erotic encounters take place: "That impossible predator, Eros the Limb-Loosener, Bitter-sweetly and afresh Savages my flesh." A wedding poem scans with these words: "May you bed down, Head to breast, upon The flesh Of a plush Companion." Sappho idealizes memories, recalling former relationships: "I loved you once, years ago, at this, when your flower was in place. You seemed a gawky girl then, artless, without grace." She can criticize a girl for not dressing properly.

Even such accessories as headscarves, handkerchiefs, baubles become status symbols: "Subtly bedizened Aphrodite, Deathless daughter of Zeus, Wile-weaver, I beg you, Empress, do not smite me with anguish and fever." She teases us by setting forth a challenge: "Some call ships, infantry, or horsemen the greatest beauty earth can offer; I say it is whatever a person most lusts after." Laughter is never too far—doing its part to cause flutters in the ventricles (cavities) of the heart. Dilated pupils signify arousal. Who can resist the command "Girls, shred your dresses"? The reward? "On a bed . . . sate your craving."[50]

I try to think what kind of a musical sound I would hear were I present when Sappho and her girls would perform. As far as I know, there are no musical notations extant. Something of what might be a similarity would be the music we have from the German abbess in the twelfth century—Hildegard von Bingen. Of course, here we would find lyrics rather different in terms of content, yet strangely similar devotionally!

Psyche (or soul) in Greek mythology was a princess so beautiful that people adored her instead of Aphrodite. To put an end to this sacrilege, Aphrodite sent her son Eros to inspire Psyche with a passion for an ugly man. Eros, however was so entranced when he saw her, dropped an arrow on her foot and fell in love with her himself.

Let's Talk about Soul

There is a song I remember singing when I was young that went like this: "I wish I had a paper doll to call my own!" We have become so visually oriented that we expect (and even provide for) certain figure images to be nearby, accessible. Most of us have a curiosity about pornography, if not a modest appreciation for it. When we think about our relationships with other people, we know that we do not really deal with them as if they were cardboard "cutups." We have enough sense to realize that each of us is a "soul" and that we have a "soul-body." We may wonder how the soul of another person manifests itself to us. Can you ferret out its presence? Would a certain kind of perception on our part be important? Some of us may be better than others in doing just this! We become conscious of what we have to work with in ourselves!

My soul, your soul, we could say, has a texture, a certain density, intensity—its own way of expressing itself! However, in terms of other people, we could be faced with our doing some detective work in order to track it down. If our love of another is worth anything, that love has become a part of ourselves, and it is there because we love the soul of this particular girlfriend, lady friend!

"Soul" has a lot to do with how we become "curators" of our own "self-image," how one "crafts" one's own life. There are a variety of feeling tones that play themselves across a broad spectrum in "soul." "Soul" often settles in the "valleys" of our lives (more often than not)—in experiences where there are "gaps"—where there have been incidents of failure, separation, loss. One becomes overtaken by a soupy mood, just drifting along! The soul responds better to some deep insight, often larded with nuance, allusion, metaphor—rather than being confronted by some bald truth. Soul enters into the cracks and crannies of our daily lives, those very interstices we attend to with negligible attention. It is in these "openings"

74

that soul may give vent to its taste for quirkiness, the perverse, and the deviant.[51] A good question to ask your loved one would be "How do you handle life's surprises or the prospect of a new experience or when you are filled with rage?" What is the difference for you between your solving a problem in the most reasonable way you can and having to live with paradox, incongruity, for months at a time? There are always things that "bother" people a lot. It can be helpful to stake them out, "put them on the table," and perhaps even celebrate them! Another question: What do you "disdain" in your own body? Given the layouts, the landscapes, in your own daily life, in what concerns do you feel the most vulnerable? What problems do you seek to sidestep or evade? What makes you get "uptight"—when you feel the need to be rigid, inflexible?

Any relationship that can bear this kind of scrutiny and weather the examination of these questions and come through them without being outraged, coming through with either joyful repentance or simply delightful laughter, in my book holds great promise and could probably turn out to be a good match.

We can, in a sense, recapitulate the facts of history *as I have done,* what warranted negative attitudes, tracking down causes that indeed lie in the anthropology of those first centuries of the Christian era. Anthropology, of course, is defined as the study of human beings in all the variety of their physical and cultural characteristics and customs, including their social relationships. It is sometimes hard to pin down the standards of this profession and the precision of what the objectivity of this work involves. This comes to a head when we compare societies whose settings are the wilds of West Africa and those in the country parts of New York State. Anthropology can include the study of cannibals, the measuring of their skulls, the initiation ceremonies into puberty of boys and girls. It is a word with slippery meanings, for it can turn into a hobby or pastime as well as a profession—especially when the curiosity it prompts ranges from scientific inquiry into "the gossipy delight of prying!" With all the card indexing and marshalling of statistical categorizing that one goes through in order to be "objective," the lot of the observer cannot help from being involved—from being detached to having his findings come at him a little too close for comfort! If we are normal people, we cannot cease from "watching one another." If we are taking upon us the role of an anthropologist, we must realize others may need to "watch us" and call us to account when we become tainted by that relentless presence of autobiography, which contains our own threads of premise, preference, and prejudice. At this point, I wish to prepare you for perusing a two-page quotation, in which there is a reference between the difference between the account of the creation of human beings in the Bible and the work of Charles Darwin, naturalist of the nineteenth century. This is taken from a book entitled *Male and Female—Christian Approaches to Sexuality* with chapter 21 on "The Sacramentality of Sex" by John W. Dixon Jr., lecturer, author, professor, at the University of North Carolina.[52] In reading just these two pages, the author gives us an accurate assessment of the ever-so-present condition of our own humanity in a "pattern" or "paradigm" form. This is a contemporary depiction in a real sense of "how we are made." This report, accounting, reminds me, actually rather emphatically, of what the Lord said to Cain in Genesis 4:7: "If you do well, will you not be accepted? And if you do not do well, sin is lurking at the door; its desire is for you, but you must master it." If what this says about us is true, then we jointly with others are meant to recognize that this is the "grid" through which we must live our lives and make those decisions in which we are seeking to achieve the abundant life. Our own awareness and consciousness of what is contained in just these two pages will go a long way in making this possible for us.

   Read slowly the following with as much concentration as you can muster.

238   John W Dixon, Jr.

The past is not distant from us but deep within us. We are different people, not as creatures transformed—caterpillar into butterfly or tadpole into frog—but as a tree adds rings. The painters of the caves are within us, the painted animals and the carved women are parts of our very selves.

We will know ourselves only as we can work back through those layers of ourselves, knowing each layer and knowing its relation to all that went before. We should not consider ourselves as travelers on a pilgrimage through time. Rather we bring essential parts of our journey with us.

As we sense ourselves so deeply involved with our past, so must we be equally involved with our bodies. Our bodies have, indeed, changed, but they too bring their past with them. Genesis and Darwin agree on the ladder of ascent or descent both spatial images of value for which I prefer the tree growing out of the center. We began in the sea, grew to reptiles to mammals to humanoids to humans, and the quality of each remains with us, only barely covered the subsequent layers. There is the cold pitiless, sub-intelligent vitality of the reptile: the passionate energy of the beast using intelligence as a tool and a weapon without moral judgment; and finally the intelligence at the service of moral decision. The tree image is almost literally present, although not quiet rendering the anatomical picture. The oldest "reptilian" brain is, in us, the brain stem at the top of the spinal column and controls those bodily functions we conceal behind the terms "automatic" and "instinctive." Folded around this knob and nearly enclosing it is the bulk of the brain, the "mammalian" brain, or rather the "paleomammalian" brain. Enclosing this brain mass is its outer surface, the neocortex.

A lot but not all is known about these brains and their functions. A few examples:

1. All people, in varying degrees have the experience of rage which or may not be controlled by will or belief.
2. Old people whose cerebral cortex has ceased to function, and the most pious people under anesthesia, will talk and behave with the grossest sexuality, entirely in conflict with the principles of their responsible lives.
3. In nations, judgment of morality and of greatness are entirely separate. In nations professing morality, the murderous tyrant is idealized as a hero, as Napoleon and Caesar have been.
4. The most reasonable and pious people have dreams of an appalling immortality. Even amateur analysis can easily uncover the powerful sexual and economic base for much of our ordinary acts.

The Sacramentality of Sex

The conclusion: our lives are under the control of distinct bodily systems. They are heirarchichally ordered; the cerebral cortex is both physically and figuratively "higher" than the brain stem and the limbic system. The higher levels can partially control the lower, but the control can be weakend or destroyed, temporarily or permanently, by chemistry, by aging, or by culture. The crocodile, the tiger, and Hitler are within us, integral parts of ourselves, ever waiting the opportunity to control the body.

How is power controlled to peace, lust to love? Not alone. Morality is generated in community, developed in community, transmitted by community. No statement I could make goes more counter to the contemporary conviction which holds that the individual is both whole and all, that each individual has an absolute right to control his or her behavior from childhood on, without control by parent, teacher, or any social force. Such conviction can only be based on the belief that morality and reason are linked within the organism and need only be left alone to develop fully. There is no evidence at all to sustain that conviction, and all evidence is against it. "The kingdom of God is within you" said Jesus, meaning the collective you—the community—or, in other words, "The kingdom of God is in the midst of you."

The conviction is not new at all; it is for us part of the nineteenth century positivism which was an outgrowth of a primitive stage of science. Too simply put, this view is that of "the ghost in the machine," a spirit or mind which is somehow separate from the body, which receives information from the body, thinks about it, and issues instructions to the body. Curious companions are found agreeing on this view of the nature of man; they differ only concerning the purposes of the instructions given to the body. The purpose may be the indulgence of the body economically or sexually, or the control of the body for some intellectual or spiritual or moral purpose. But, whatever the different purposes, the analysis is the same; the ascetic and the licentious agree, the bank president and the hippie are brothers underneath their stated purpose, because they act on the same image of the human.

Yet we are not all related to the world in that way. It is now necessary to describe still a third hierarchical structure making up our way of being. The first of these in my account of them was the growth of the human psyche historically, successive of self's development. The second was the hierarchical ordering of the nervous system from the brain stem (and its attendant nervous system) to the cerebral cortex. The third is the system of relations between these two. The keyword now is "patterns" or "paradigm" or "model."

My Startings, My Impulses,
My Coming In, My Going Out

It is not unusual for us to turn to the Bible for help when we find we are having difficulty fighting the battle of life. There are texts that are referenced for us in many books of devotion—depending on the specifics of our need. It would seem that there would surely be something "there" for a young person having difficulty with the insistence of his (or her) own sexuality. For many of us who perhaps even long ago weathered the wild imaginings of adolescence, we can recall—sometimes vividly—those times when the penis would strike out with a life of its own. Because scripture for the most part has a reticence even to mention such a thing in the same way we have, it does require some effort on our part to ransack what might avail, what might pinpoint specific guidance. When a relationship of love, affection, prevails between a couple, and they find themselves "thrown together," their desire to express this escalates and often comes as an intrusion into a setting in which much else is going on—it is an intrusion, but a welcome one at that. The question arises as to how this is handled! Might it be possible to earmark the kind of prayer that is offered to God on such an occasion? In my opinion, the best approach for such an emotional crisis is found in Psalm 139. A few lines of quotation are in order here:

> "Lord, you have searched me out and know me; you know my
> sitting down and my rising up; you discern my thought from afar.
> You trace my journeys and my resting places and are acquainted
> with all my ways . . . You press upon me behind and before and
> lay your hand upon me. Such knowledge is too wonderful for
> me; it is so high that I cannot attain to it. Where can I go then
> from your Spirit? Where can I flee from your presence?"

Then follows several lines of the author wondering what options might be open simply to escape from the presence of God. The point is made that wherever we are however much we may seek to hide ourselves, God is with us intimately. He beholds us and does not cease in holding us, letting us go! For him, "darkness and light to him are both alike." There is further revelation—beyond the recognition that he created us. He also determined how we were to develop given our original bodily frame.

> "For you yourself created my inmost parts; you knit me together in my mother's womb . . . My body was not hidden from you, while I was being made in secret and woven in the depths of the earth. Your eyes beheld my limbs, yet unfinished in the womb; all of them were written in your book . . ."

There in verse 22, the author prays,

> "Search me out, O God, and know my heart; try me and know my restless thoughts . . ."

This Psalm reflects certain ambivalence by the author about God having such intimate knowledge of himself and of every other living human being. Nothing is hidden—even in the deepest recesses of both mind and imagination. The "self" is very transparent—including thoughts as well as spoken words. The Spirit's curious circumlocutions over the face of the earth bespeak God's active presence in the universe. Images of God as Weaver, Potter, are here set forth, factoring in the process of development is for the author an intimacy at once glorious, but almost unbearable. In the midst of this cosmic inclusiveness, the poet experiences the Lord as enfolding him, touching him, healing him. I have been helped in our focus upon this concern by the little book entitled *The Private Devotions of Lancelot Andrews* who lived from 1555 to 1626. He was a noted preacher, an unrivaled scholar, and a Bible translator, who drank deeply from the historical reservoir of Christian prayer. In a pattern of short phrases, he amplifies what we would commend to God in this Psalm—"my impulses, and my startings, my intentions, and my attempts, my going out and my coming in, my sitting down and my rising up."[53] I have added several more that I need to give an account of—my flights of fancy, my scary fantasies, my perfunctory rigidities, and my abject provocations.

Sometimes the things that are true of us, about us, we are not fully aware. It is in the midst of a loving relationship, where things become intense, there comes a time when we first need to admit to ourselves that it would be appropriate for us to declare where we are coming from. At this point, for example, the one partner could say to the other, "I feel it meaningful to tell you in the context of the ongoing relationship we have with one another that I would like to make love to you!" Surely, this is an invitation that calls for first of a response, and it can play dangerously into the dreams and hopes of his lady friend, who has cultivated for years the desire for years that someday her Prince Charming will come along and take possession of her. Yet were someone she likes getting to know to present himself to her in a moment of passion, it would be too overwhelming and frightening—to say the least. Yet it is within this very contest that the validity of sounding out, probing, seeking to ascertain the mutuality of feelings, would not be a falsification of love's expression. It could be a respectable offer that would be deserving of a meaningful reply!

Endnotes

All references to the Bible are from the Revised Standard Version and are found "online" in the text of the written document itself. Works cited in the endnotes are found in the bibliography.

1. Mary MacDerrmott Shideler, *The Theology of Romantic Love*: A Study in the Writings of Charles Williams, pages 1-42.
2. Thomas T Harding, *The Novels of Charles Williams*, page 1-21.
3. *Ibid.*, page 11-13.
4. Shideler, op. cit., pages 11-12 and 63-70.
5. C. S. Lewis, *The Four Loves*, page 140.
6. Rhonda Byrne, *The Secret*, pages 113-140.
7. Monica Furlong, *Traveling In*, pages 65ff.
8. "Intimations of Immortality," *Romantic Poetry of the Early 19th Century*, page 77.
9. John Donne, Elegie 19 "Going to Bed," *The Poems of John Donne*, page 107.
10. Charles Williams, *Essential Writings*, pages 68-90, also, Shideler, op. cit., pages 29-42.
11. *The New Oxford Book of English Verse*, page 240.
12. Shideler, op. cit., page 37.
13. Shideler, op. cit., page 39.
14. *The New Interpreter's Study Bible*, page 953.
15. Marcia Falk, *The Song of Songs*, Preface xii-xxii.
16. Daphne Merkin, "The Woman in the Balcony-On Rereading The Song of Songs" in *Out of the Garden*, pages 238-251.
17. Phyllis Trible, *God and the Rhetoric of Sexuality*, pages 149-165.
18. Michael R. Cosby, *Sex in the Bible*, pages 54-81.
19. Elizabeth Barrett Browning, *Sonnets from the Portuguese,* xiv page 13.

20. Rollo May, *Love and Will*, pages 45-63.

21. Thomas Mann, *Joseph and His Brothers*, pages 748-757.

22. *Book of Common Prayer*, page 216.

23. John O'Donohue, *Beauty the Invisible Embrace*, pages 152-158.

24. *The Wisdom of Israel*, page 239.

25. *The New Interpreter's Study Bible*, page 1755.

26. *The Woman's Bible Commentary*, page 255.

27. *Preaching Through the Christian Year*, pages 114, 115.

28. Wayne G. Robbins, *Jung and the Bible*, pages 26-33.

29. Matthew Fox, *Sins of the Spirit, Blessings of the Flesh*, pages 208-217.

30. *The Book of Common Prayer*, page 301-303.

31. Lines from "Tintern Abbey," *Romantic Poetry of the Early Nineteenth Century*, page 48.

32. Samuel Coleridge Taylor. *Romantic Poetry of the Early Nineteenth Centur*, pages 118-121.

33. Stephen Prickett, *Romanticism, and Religion The Tradition of Coleridge and Wordsworth in the Victorian Church*, page 240.

34. Alfred Kazin, Ed. *The Portable Blake*, pages 14-16, and "*The Marriage of Heaven and Hell*" pages 250-260.

35. *Reader's Encyclopedia*, page 576.

36. Juliet Barker, *The Bronte's*, page 721-808.

37. Susan Chitty, *The Beast and the Monk*, especially chapters-"The Lonely Curate" pages 65-78 and "*The Lover for all Eternity*" pages 79-86.

38. Harold C. Gardiner, Editor. *The Imitation of Christ*, Introduction pages 5-19.

39. John Worthen *D. H. Lawrence-The Life of an Outsider*, chapter 9 "Sons and Lovers and Marriage" pages 125-147, and chapter 14 "Ending With Love" pages 229-250, and chapter 23 "Lady Chatterley's Lover, 1927-1928" pages 364-374.

40. Rabbi Eckstein, *How Firm a Foundation*, pages 136-139.

41. Bonnell Spencer, *God Who Dares to be Man*, pages 86-98.

42. *The Spiritual Exercises of St. Ignatius*, pages 21, 31, 40.

43. "Buddha" in *Reader's Encyclopedia*, page 137.

44. Karen Armstrong, *Mohammed*, pages 229-240.

45. Robertson Davies, *Fifth Business*, page 176, 177.

46. Frederick Buechner, *Wishful Thinking*-"Myth," page 65.

47. Wayne G. Robbins, *Jung and the Bible*, page 27-33.

48. Poem in *Earth Prayers From Around the World*, page 187.

49. Ginettte Paris, *Pagan Meditations*, pages 11-105.

50. *Sappho, Stung with Love*: Poems, Fragments, also Ginette Paris, *Pagan Meditations*, pages 37-62.

51. Thomas Moore, *Care of the Soul*, especially pages 1-136.

52. *Ibid.*, pages referenced-238, 239.

53. *The Private Devotions of Lancelot Andrews*, pages 23, 24.

Illustrations

1. Frontispiece, *The Sleeping Congregation* by William Hogarth 1697-1764 The Victorian Clergyman by Trevor May, Shire Publications Ltd. Buckinghamshire HP27 AA UK.
2. *Birth of Venus* (Aphrodite)—Sandro Botticilli, Wikipedia the free Encyclopedia.
3. *The Three Graces of Charities* by Raphael, Wikipedia the free Encyclopedia.
4. *Cupid and Psyche* by Francois Gerad 1798, Wikipedia the free Encyclopedia.

Bibliography

Alda, Alan. *Things Overheard While Talking to Myself* (New York: Mayflower Productions, Inc. Random House Inc., 2007)

Amplified New Testament The (Grand Rapids, Michigan: Zondervan Publishing House, 1958)

Aphrodits, Artemis, and Hestia (Dallas, Texas: Spring Publications, Inc., 1986)

Armstrong, Karen. *Muhammad A. Biography of the Prophet* (New York: Harper Collins Publishers, 1993)

Barker, Juliet. *The Brontes* (New York: St. Martin's Press 1994)

Barnhouse, Ruth Tiffany and Holmes, Urban T. *Male and Female Christian Approaches to Sexuality* (New York: A Crossroad Book, The Seabury Press 1976)

Beatty, Arthur. *Romantic Poetry of the Early Nineteenth Century*(New York: Charles Scribner's Sons 1928)

Benet's Readers Encyclopedia (New York: Harper and Row, Publishers, 1965)

Book of Common Prayer The and Administration of the Sacraments and other Rites. Ceremonies of the Church (New York: Oxford University Press. 1990)

Browne, Lewis, Editor. *The Wisdom of Israel* (New York: The Modern Library, Random House, Inc. 1945)

Buechner, Frederick. *Wishful Thinking* A Theological ABC (New York: Harper Collins Publishers. 1973)

Buchman, Christina, Spiegel, Celina, Editors. *Out of the Garden Women Writers on the Bible* (New York: Fawcett Columbine Book Ballantine Books, Random House, Inc. 1994)

Byrne, Rhonda. *The Secret* (New York: Beyond Words Publishing. Atria Books, 2006)

Chitty, Susan. *The Beast and the Monk, A Life of Charles Kingsley* (New York: Mason/Charter Publishers, 1974)

Cosby, Michael R. *Sex in the Bible*. An Introduction, (Englewood Cliffs, New Jersey: Prentice Hall, Inc. 1984)

Craddock, Fred B. Prof., others. *Preaching Through The Christian Year*. Year A (Harrisburg. Pa., Trinity Press International, 1992)

Davies, Robertson. *Fifth Business* (New York: Penguin Books, 1970)

Eckstein, Rabbi Yechiel. *How Firm a Foundation a Gift of Jewish Wisdom for Christians and Jews* (Brewster, Ma.: Paraclete Press, 1999)

Falk, Marcia. *The Song of Songs A New Translation* (San Francisco: Harper Collins Publishers 1990)

Furlong, Monica. *Traveling In* (Cincinnati, Ohio: Forward Movement Miniature Book, 1972)

Ganns, George E., S. J., Translator. *The Spiritual Exerciser of St. Ignatius* (Chicago: Loyola University Press, 1992)

Gardiner, Harold C. Editor. *The Imitations of Christ* A Modern Version. (Garden City, New York: Image Books, Doubleday and Co., Inc., 1955)

Gardner, Helen, Editor. *The New Oxford Book of English Verse* 1250-1950 (New York: Oxford University Press 1972)

Grierson, H. J. C. Editor. *The Poems of John Ionne* (London: Oxford University Press. 1945)

Hefling, Charles, Ed. *Charles Williams Essential Writings*, (Boston, Ma. Cowley Publications, 1993)

Holmes, Nancy, Selector. *Sonnets From the Portuguese* Poems of Elizabeth Barrett Browning (Kansas City, Missouri: Hallmark Cards. Inc., 1967)

Holy Bible The with the Apocryphal/Deuterocanonical Books. New Revised Standard Version (New York: Oxford University Press. 1989)

Howard, Thomas T. *The Novels of Charles Williams* (New York: Oxford University Press, 1983)

Kazin, Alfred, Introducer. *The Portable Blake* (New York Penguin Books, 1974)

Kepler, Thomas S. Editor and Intro. *The Private Devotions of Lancelot Andrews* (New York: The World Publishing Company, 1956)

Lawrence, D. H. *The Rainbow* (New York: Modern Library Paperback Edition, Random House, Inc., 2002)

Lawrence, D. H. *Sons and Lovers* (New York: Barnes and Noble Classics, with New Introduction, 2003)

Lewis, C. S. *The Four Loves* (New York: Harcourt Brace Jovanovich, Inc., 1960)

Liturgy of the Church of England The, The Book of Common Prayer, (London: John Basket, Printer 1727)

Mann, Thomas. *Joseph and His Brothers* (New York: Borzoi Book Alfred A. Knopf, Inc., 1963)

May, Rollo. *Love and Will* (New York: W.W. Norton and Co. Inc., 1969)

Moore, Thomas. *Care of the Soul a Guide For Cultivating Depth and Sacredness in Everyday Life* New York: Harper Collins Publishers, 1992)

New Interpreter's Study Bible The New Revised Standard Version with the Apocrypha (Nashville, Tn., 2003)

Newsom, Carol A., Ringe, Sharon H., Editors. *The Women's Bible Commentary* (Louisville. Ky. Westminster/John Knox Press,1992)

O'Donohue, John. *Beauty The Invisible Embrace* (New York: Harper Collins Publishers, 2004)

Ohanneson, Joan. *Scarlet Music Hildegard of Bingen—A Novel* (New York: The Crossroad Publishing Co., 1998)

Paris, Ginette (Translation from the French) *Pagan Meditations, The Worlds of*

Poochigan, Aaron. Translator and Intro. *Sappho Stung With Love: Poems and Fragments*(New York, Penguin Group, 2009)

Prickett, Stephen. *Romanticism and Religion The Tradition of Coleridge and Wordsworth*

Richards, J. A. Editor. *The Portable Coleridge* (New York: Penguin Books, 1978)

Roberts, Elizabeth and Amidon, Elias. Editors, *Earth Prayers from Around the World* (New York: Harper Collins Publishers, 1991)

Rollins, Wallace Eugene and Rollins, Marion Benedect. *Jesus and His Ministry* (Greenwich, Conn.: The Seabury Press, 1954)

Rollins, Wayne Gilbert. *Jung and the Bible* (Atlanta Georgia: John Knox Press. 1983) Fox, Matthew. *Sins of the Spirit, Blessings of the Flesh* (New York: Three Rivers Press, Crown Publishing Group Random House, Inc.,1999)

Shideler, Mary Mac Dermott. *The Theology of Romantic Love*: A Study in the Writings of Charles Williams (Grand Rapids, Michigan, Eerdmans Pub. Co. 1962)

Spencer, Bonnell. *God Who Dares to be Man* Theology for Prayer and Suffering (New York: Seabury Press. 1980)

Spong, John Shelby. *Born of a Woman* (New York: Harper Collins Publishers, 1992)

Trible, Phyllis. *God and the Rhetoric of Sexuality* (Philadelphia: Fortress Press, 1978)

Ultimate Encyclopedia of Mythology The (London, Hermes House, 2005)

Worthen, John. *D.H. Lawrence The Life of an Outsider* (Cambridge, Ma: Counterpoint: Perseus Books Group, 2005)

Breinigsville, PA USA
18 January 2011
253580BV00002B/10/P

9 781456 836610